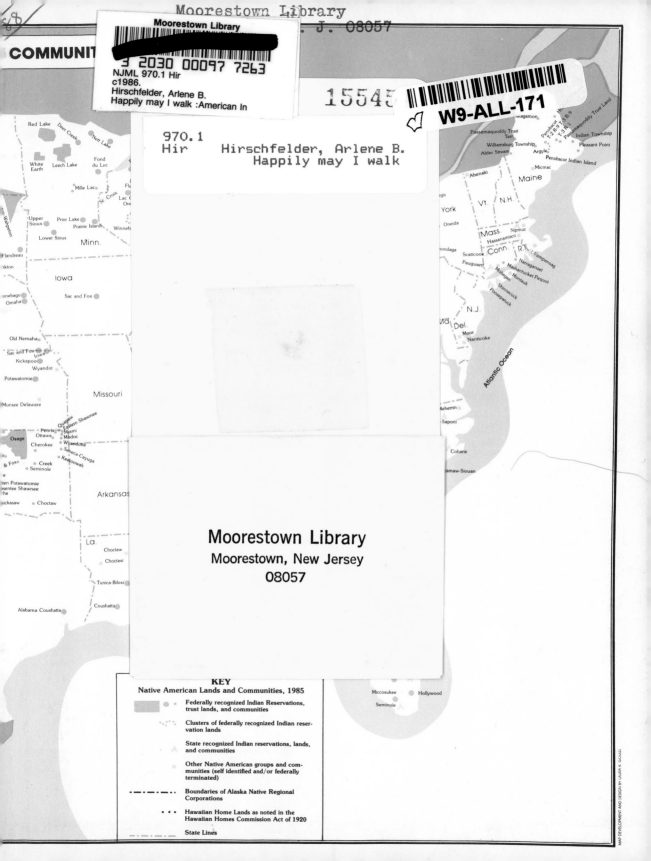

COMMUNIT

15545

W9-ALL-171

KEY
Native American Lands and Communities, 1985

Federally recognized Indian Reservations, trust lands, and communities

Clusters of federally recognized Indian reservation lands

State recognized Indian reservations, lands, and communities

Other Native American groups and communities (self identified and/or federally terminated)

Boundaries of Alaska Native Regional Corporations

Hawaiian Home Lands as noted in the Hawaiian Homes Commission Act of 1920

State Lines

MAP DEVELOPMENT AND DESIGN BY LAURA K. GOULD

HAPPILY
MAY I WALK

HAPPILY MAY I WALK

◇ ◇ ◇

American Indians and Alaska Natives Today

◇ ◇ ◇

ARLENE HIRSCHFELDER

CHARLES SCRIBNER'S SONS · NEW YORK

To Mary Gloyne Byler, for her years of sharing

A portion of the author's royalties will be donated to Fort Totten Convalescent Home of the Devils Lake Sioux Tribe, North Dakota

The author acknowledges with thanks the contributions of photographers Pena Bonita, Paul S. Conklin, Joseph C. Farber, John C. Goodwin, George Hight, Elizabeth Lenell, Kenneth B. Metoxen, Nelson Navarro, and Virgil J. Vogel, the Bureau of Indian Affairs, The Museum of the American Indian, and the Native American Science Education Association.

Charles Scribner's Sons Books for Young Readers
Macmillan Publishing Company
866 Third Avenue, New York, NY 10022
Collier Macmillan Canada, Inc.

Printed in the United States of America
First Edition
10 9 8 7 6 5 4 3 2 1

Library of Congress Cataloging-in-Publication Data
Hirschfelder, Arlene B.   Happily may I walk.
Bibliography: p.   Includes index.
1. Indians of North America—Juvenile literature.   I. Title.
E77.4.H56 1986   970.00497   85-43349
ISBN 0-684-18624-1

Happily may I walk.

Happily, with abundant dark clouds, may I walk.

Happily, with abundant showers, may I walk.

Happily, with abundant plants, may I walk.

Happily, on a trail of pollen, may I walk.

Happily may I walk.

Being as it used to be long ago, may I walk.

May it be beautiful before me.

May it be beautiful behind me.

May it be beautiful below me.

May it be beautiful above me.

May it be beautiful all around me.

In beauty it is finished.

from "A Prayer of the Night Chant"

Navajo Myths, Prayers, and Songs, compiled by Washington Matthews. Berkeley, CA: University of California Publications in American Archaeology and Ethnology, Vol. 5, 1907.

Contents

Introduction

American Indians do not have red skin, painted faces, or feathers on their heads. Eskimos in Alaska did not live in snow igloos. All of these notions are stereotypes, over-simplified pictures about a particular group, race, or sex. A stereotype usually is negative and prevents us from knowing groups of people as they truly are. Stereotypes block us from seeing people as unique and special.

This book, containing new information about the ways Native Americans live in the United States today, has been written to help you "unlearn" Indian stereotypes.

America's Native peoples are Indians, Eskimos, and Aleuts. Most Eskimos and Aleuts live in Alaska, while most Indians live in the "lower forty-eight," the phrase Alaskans use to refer to the continental United States. But there are also Indians living in Alaska, and Eskimos and Aleuts living all over the country.

When Columbus reached America he thought he was in India, so he called the people he met "Indians," a name that has stuck to this day. Sometimes we use "Native American" to refer to all Indians, Eskimos, and Aleuts. Sometimes we use "American Indian" or "Indian" or "Native people" when we are talking about more than one tribe at a time. If possible, one should use the proper name of a tribe rather than general terms.

Before the time of Columbus, a person would never have said, "I am an Indian." He or she would have said "I am a Hopi" or "I am a Kiowa" or "I am a Penobscot." People identified themselves by the tribe they belonged to. Today people still prefer to identify themselves by their tribal affiliation rather than as Indians.

The names most Native American people use to refer to their tribes are different from the names outsiders use. Some of the people we know as Sioux prefer to be called *Lakota*, which means "allies" in the Siouan language. Some of the people we call Navajo prefer to be called *Diné*, which means "the people" in the Athabascan language. Some Chippewas prefer to be called *Anishinabe*, which means "woodland people" in the Algonquian language.

In 1985 members of the Papago tribe announced plans to change their name to *Tohono O'odham Nation*, which means "the desert people." Tribal leaders no longer wish to be called Papago, a Spanish corruption of an Indian word for "bean eaters."

Many people we call Eskimo prefer to call themselves *Inuit*, meaning "the people" in the Inuit language. The word Eskimo does not belong to the Inuit language; it is a term used by Indians and means "eaters of raw meat."

Most tribal people have gradually been forced to accept names invented for them by non-Indians. In this book, both the tribal names that people prefer and the invented names will be used interchangeably.

In the United States, there is no one definition of an Indian. Some full-blooded Indians do not consider Indians with one-quarter Indian heritage to be Indian, while other people with very little Indian blood consider themselves Indian. Most tribal groups call a person with at least one-fourth tribal heritage a member, but some tribes insist on one-half tribal blood and others list members with $\frac{1}{128}$ Indian heritage. The Census Bureau lists as Indian those people who say they are. The Bureau of Indian Affairs, the main federal agency that works with Indian people, recognizes as Indian those people who live on or near a reservation, are members of a tribe the government calls a tribe, and have at least one-fourth Indian blood. One Indian law center has recorded fifty-two definitions of Indians used in law.

Indians are *not* alike. The Navajos of Arizona and the Mohawks of New York are as different from each other as the French and Chinese. Although tribes are worlds apart in many cultural ways, they share certain beliefs, including the view that land has a spiritual meaning.

In 1890, the Indian, Eskimo, and Aleut population was 273,000. By 1960, the population had jumped to 552,000. In 1970, the Native American population was 763,594, and in 1980, the Census Bureau counted 1,418,195 Indians, Inuits, and Aleuts. Of this total, 717,188 are female. The Native American population is younger in age than the national population. About thirty-one percent of the Native population is under fifteen years of age in contrast to almost twenty-three percent of the national population. Only seven and a half percent of the Indian population is over sixty years old while almost sixteen percent of the general population is sixty and older.

Today, less than one half of the American Indian, Inuit, and Aleut population lives on reservations and in Alaska Native villages. More than one half of the population lives in cities and rural areas all over the United States. California has the largest Indian, Inuit, and Aleut population with 201,311 counted in 1980. Vermont has the smallest, 984.

Native Americans are citizens of the United States *and* members of Indian tribes. In 1924, U.S. citizenship was granted to all Indians born in the United States.

Native Americans have joined all other Americans in defending the United States against enemies. In World War I, even before Indians were granted citizenship, 12,000 Indian men and women served in the military forces. Nearly all were volunteers. In World War II, 25,000 Indians served. They were awarded seventy-one Air Medals, fifty-one

Silver Stars, forty-seven Bronze Stars, thirty-four Distinguished Flying Crosses, and two Congressional Medals of Honor. In the Vietnam War, over 42,500 Indians fought in Southeast Asia in the Army, Navy, Marines, and Air Force.

Several hundred Navajo Indians made history as "Code Talkers" in the Marine Corps during World War II. They used the Navajo language as the basis for a military code, transmitting messages in combat zones throughout the Pacific Ocean. The Japanese never broke the code. To honor the Navajos who served, Congress and the President declared August 14, 1982, "Navajo Code Talkers' Day."

Indian men and women have been elected to government office for over seventy years. Charles Curtis, Kaw Indian from Oklahoma, was vice-president under President Hoover. Indians have been elected to Congress, state, city, and local governments and school boards.

In 1492, Indians owned (that is, used) almost two billion acres of land. Today, Indian lands total around fifty million acres in the lower forty-eight, and Alaska Natives have title to around forty-four million acres of land—nearly five percent of the United States.

Like all citizens, Indians must pay federal income taxes, but not on money they earn using their own lands. If Indians grow crops or sell timber or minerals from their lands, for example, they do not have to pay federal taxes on the money received from the sales. Indians do not pay state taxes on anything purchased within reservation boundaries. In practice, many Indians live, work, and do most of their shopping off reservations, so they escape few taxes.

The chapters that follow will tell you a great deal more about the everyday life of American Indians and Alaska Natives today, especially their efforts to maintain their ancient cultures.

1

Tribal Governments

The word "tribe" has many meanings. A tribe is a group of people having a common cultural ancestry who speak the same language, share a history that stretches far back in time, and have the same religion, traditions, and values. Members of a tribe look at the world in the same way. A tribe is also a political group. Members live within a certain area, today called a reservation, in a community under a tribal government. Tribes have sovereignty, the right of self-government.

There are over 400 Indian tribes in the United States. The Navajo is the largest. In 1980, there were some 172,000 Navajos, about 132,000 living on reservation land, 20,000 in the immediate area surrounding Navajo land, and 20,000 living in distant cities. The Oglala Sioux is the second largest *reservation* tribe, with 12,000 members living on the Pine Ridge Sioux Reservation and many more in cities. (The Cherokee Nation of Oklahoma is the second largest *non-reservation* tribe. In 1980, the tribe had over 23,000 members.) In 1980, eight tribes had more than 5,000 members living on reservations: the Blackfeet of Montana; the Fort Apache, Gila River, Hopi, Papago, and San Carlos Apache all in Arizona; the Rosebud Sioux of South Dakota; and Zuni Pueblo of New Mexico. Over two hundred tribes have fewer than 1,000 people living on reservations.

Sometimes the government views two or more tribes who speak different languages but share a reservation as one tribe politically. The Fort Belknap Indian community in Montana, for example, is considered one tribe, though it is composed of two culturally different tribes, the Gros Ventres and the Assiniboines. The Wind River Tribes (Shoshone and Arapahoe) in Wyoming are considered one tribe. The Three Affiliated Tribes of Fort Berthold (Mandan, Hidatsa, and Arikara) in North Dakota are treated as one tribe, as are the Salish and Kutenai Tribes on the Flathead Reservation in Montana.

On the other hand, a single tribe divided into a number of groups living on different reservations is sometimes considered different tribes from a political point of view. The Yanktonai Sioux on the Standing Rock Reservation in South Dakota and those on the Devil's Lake Sioux Reservation in North Dakota are treated by the government as separate tribes.

Long before Europeans came to this country, Indian people living in present-day United States were independent and self-governing. They managed their own affairs, had their own unwritten legal systems, and

John C. Goodwin, United Methodist Board of Global Ministries

Road sign tells drivers they are about to enter the Pine Ridge Reservation, home of the Oglala Sioux Indian Tribe

dealt with other Indian nations. Tribes lost most of their external powers after they were subjected to U.S. authority. Today they are not allowed to make treaties or establish political connections with any nations outside the United States. A few internal powers of tribes have also been limited. Tribes may not sell tribal trust lands without the government's permission—a regulation intended to protect reservation lands—nor arrest and prosecute criminals for certain crimes. Even with such limitations, however, Indian tribes have a great deal of power to regulate reservation activities and the behavior of tribal members.

The U.S. Constitution provides for a republican form of government, for separation of powers into three branches of government, and for the separation of church and state. These constitutional ideas do *not* apply to tribes. Tribes have the right to choose and operate their own form of government. Tribes decide what kind of governments best fit their needs. This often depends on their cultural, historical, and religious traditions.

Many tribes now have written constitutions patterned after the U.S. Constitution. Many have three branches like the federal and state governments—executive, legislative, and judicial—but some have other types of government. Some pueblos in New Mexico operate under an ancient system called a theocracy. Priests select pueblo governors and other officials who manage the routine affairs of the pueblos. These supreme priests are called *Kikmongwi* in the Hopi Pueblo, *Pekwin* in the Zuni Pueblo, *Xwivela* in the Jemez Pueblo, and so on. They hold their positions for life. Other pueblos elect their officials by ballots and have a constitutional form of government.

The Nipmucs of Massachusetts are governed by a chairman and board of directors. Members over eighteen years of age may serve on the board. The Miccosukees of Florida have a governing body composed of four matrilineal clans (a group of families related through the women) and a business committee composed of one member from each clan.

Around 200 tribes have governing bodies called councils. Some governing bodies are called business committees, or business councils, or executive committees. Most tribal officials are elected for two-, three-, or four-year terms. In most tribes, council members are elected; in others they are appointed by elders.

Some tribes call their leaders chairman, some president. The Pueblos call their leaders governor. The Creeks of Oklahoma call their leaders principal chiefs.

The Navajo Tribe has the country's largest governing body. In the mid-1980s, it had an eighty-seven-member tribal council, elected every four years by popular vote of the Navajo people on the reservation.

In recent years, Indian women have become more involved in tribal political systems. In 1982, fifty-nine women headed tribes and Alaska Native villages and corporations.

For centuries, tribes have made the rules that determine membership and have kept written rolls of members. A few tribes have the right to take tribal membership away from a person.

Tribal requirements for membership vary. As we have seen, many groups require a minimum of one-quarter tribal blood, others require as much as one-half. A few tribes permit any descendant of a tribal member to be enrolled regardless of the degree of tribal blood. Some tribes require that people be born on the reservation or live on it for a certain length of time before they can apply for membership. Several pueblos in New Mexico allow children of mixed marriages to become members if the father is a pueblo member. Other groups have ruled that only descendants of female members of the tribe can be members.

The federal government also decides who are members of tribes. Congress creates Indian programs and decides who can participate. Sometimes, the government uses tribal membership rolls. Other times, programs include only people with one-quarter or more tribal blood.

Tribal councils have the power to make laws that regulate everyday life, including marriage, divorce, and child adoptions. Tribes have education committees, housing authorities, legislative committees, and law and order committees. They have the right to maintain law and order among their members and to punish members who break laws. They have police forces, courts, and jails.

Tribes have the right to tax their members, the same right the federal and state governments have to tax their citizens. This power to tax is at the heart of self-government, for without the ability to raise money to support tribal programs, self-government is not possible. Tribes can tax non-Indians using tribal lands for farming and grazing. They can tax the oil and gas extracted by non-Indian companies operating on reservations, and they can regulate fishing and hunting on their homelands. Tribes can exclude trespassers from tribal territory and can regulate the use of reservation property among tribal members and non-Indians. (The U.S. government requires non-Indian traders to obtain permits from tribal governments before they open businesses on reservations.) Tribes are beginning to impose land use ordinances in an attempt to preserve and protect their land.

Tribal courts decide civil disputes between Indians and non-Indians on reservations. A civil dispute is one that involves ordinary, private matters that are not unlawful. Tribal courts largely deal with divorce, child custody problems, civil disputes between Indian citizens, and minor crimes such as violations of fishing regulations. Federal law enforcers handle major crimes such as murder, arson, burglary, and robbery. Tribal courts cannot impose more than a $500 penalty or a jail sentence longer than six months in criminal cases.

Courts differ from reservation to reservation. Some judges are elected to their positions; others are appointed by the tribe. Indians use English in most tribal courts. Occasionally, older Indians use their tribal language, and some judges respond in the same language. Court proceedings on the Navajo Reservation are conducted in the Navajo language, in English, or in a mixture of both languages.

9

❖ 2 ❖

Reservations

A reservation is a piece of land that belongs to one or more groups of American Indians. There are hundreds of federal and state Indian reservations located in thirty-five states in our country. Reservations are not public property like parks, and they are not part of the states surrounding them. Reservations have definite boundary lines just like states. These lines separate reservations from the states in which they are located.

The word "reservation" dates from the 1800s when the U.S. army drove Indians into small corners of their lands or drove them off their homelands altogether. Indians had owned their lands for thousands of years. In the nineteenth century, the U.S. government forced them to settle on lands "reserved" for their use, parts of their own lands or of another tribe's lands.

Many reservations were created by written treaties until 1871, when Congress prohibited the making of treaties with Indians. After that time, many reservations were created by Executive Order of the President and by other kinds of arrangements. In return for giving up large parts of their ancestral homelands, the Indians were to receive schools, medical care, and other services.

In 1980, the Census Bureau counted about 300 federal and state American Indian reservations, some of which are shared by two or three tribes. Most of these reservations—almost 200—are in western states. Fifty-two reservations are located in midwestern states, eighteen are in northeastern states, and sixteen are in southern states. California alone has over 100 reservations. Washington State has twenty-six reservations; Arizona has twenty; and Alaska, South Carolina, Mississippi, and Iowa each have one. In 1985, fifteen states did not have any federal or state Indian reservation lands.

Some reservations cross state boundaries, like the Navajo Reservation that covers parts of Arizona, New Mexico, and Utah. The Sac and Fox Reservation is located in parts of Kansas and Nebraska.

Reservations come in all sizes. The Navajo Reservation, the largest in the United States, has almost sixteen million acres of land, the size of Costa Rica or West Virginia. The O'odham (Papago) Reservation in Arizona is the second biggest with close to three million acres. Nine other reservations have more than one million acres. Three are in Arizona, two in Washington State and South Dakota, one in Wyoming, and another in Montana.

Most reservations are much smaller. Almost one hundred reservations are under one thousand acres, and some are specks compared to the largest reservation. The Golden Hill (Paugusset Indians) Reservation in Connecticut, the smallest in the country, is one-quarter of an acre.

There are important natural resources on reservations. The Blackfeet, Crow, and Fort Peck Reservations in Montana and the Wind River Reservation in Wyoming have large deposits of oil and gas. The Navajo Reservation contains some of the richest coal and uranium deposits in the southwestern part of the country. The Metlakatla (Tsimpshian Indians) Reservation in Alaska has valuable forest lands.

Non-Indians can pay Indians for the right to live on and use reservation lands to farm, to graze cattle, to harvest timber. The Agua Calientes of southern California lease part of their reservation lands to stores, hotels, office buildings, apartments, and country clubs in the heart of Palm Springs. Even the Palm Springs post office is located on Agua Caliente land.

Most of the town of Salamanca, New York, leases reservation land from the Seneca Nation.

It is possible for non-Indians to own land on reservations. The General Allotment Act of 1887 broke up some tribal lands into allotments or plots of 160 acres, and some individual Indians have sold off their allotments to non-Indians.

In many ways, Indian people who live on reservations spend time doing things just like Americans everywhere. Indian children wear designer jeans, go to school and to the movies, listen to music, play baseball, and ride bikes. Indian adults go to work in offices, grow crops, raise cattle.

In other ways Indian reservations are special places. On Indian lands, young and old are members of families that make up a community that shares a language, a history, religious traditions and practices. Family members feel responsible for one another and support their relatives in good times and bad times.

On reservations, Indian children, like children everywhere, learn the most important things about their culture from their parents, neighbors, and religious and political leaders. They learn to speak the language of their ancestors. They participate in community ceremonies and feasts. They learn how to behave by watching adults and by listening to their grandparents tell them stories about their tribe's customs and traditions. They watch medicine men or women perform healing ceremonies for sick people and sometimes decide to become medicine men or women. They watch the artists of the tribe create baskets, rugs, jewelry, or wood carvings of great beauty and learn to do these things.

Native Americans have reverence and respect for the land, which some call "Mother Earth," and they treat their reservation lands with great care. Many feel that if they hurt the earth, it will die and that animals, plants, and eventually people will die as well. This belief helps to explain why Indians are angry when their reservation lands are taken from them and ruined. Some Cherokee lands in Tennessee were flooded to make recreational lakes for non-Indians. The Oahe Dam in South Dakota ruined more Indian lands than any other public work project in America; it flooded 160,889 acres on Standing Rock Reservation and Cheyenne River Reservation (both Sioux reserves), destroying rangelands, gardens, farms, timber, wild fruit, and wildlife resources.

Although they seldom exercise it, every Indian tribe has the right to decide who may enter its reservation and who must leave. Many tribes want visitors to come to their lands. Dozens of tribes own or operate resorts, hotels, motels, and campgrounds for tourists. The Havasupai Indians of Arizona own a twenty-four-unit lodge in the Havasu Canyon; the tribes of the Warm Springs Reservation in Oregon have built the Kah-Nee-Ta Resort, which offers swimming pools, a golf course, and twenty-one tipis that each sleep up to ten youngsters. The resort's motto is "Not just another resort, another culture."

Visitors are guests when they visit Indian reservations and must obey regulations and customs of the tribes. The Havasupai Tribe, located at the bottom of the Grand Canyon in Arizona, requires visitors to get permission to visit certain parts of the reservation. The tribe instructs people how to act in those areas that have great religious meaning to the tribe. The Hopis of Arizona do not want visitors to photograph, record, or sketch in any of the villages on the reservation. On other reservations, there are signs that tell visitors where they may and may not go.

In this century, large numbers of American Indians have moved from their reservations to cities. Many have nevertheless held on to their tribal identities and traditions, and they return to their reservations to attend tribal ceremonies and social gatherings called powwows. They return to be with their relatives and friends and to be on the land from which they came.

Years ago, an Apache girl explained why a reservation is so impor-

13

tant to Indians, whether they are living there or somewhere else:

A reservation is a source of security to the Indian. I say this because there he can feel free—freedom in practicing his own customs. Another thing is his land. . . . his land is his own. His ancestors inhabited that land; he was brought up on that land; he knows it; he claims it. What if the reservations were abolished? Then . . . the Indian would be "lost."

3

Alaska Natives

The term Alaska Natives refers to some 64,000 Inuit, Indian, and Aleut people who live in Alaska, in about 200 Native villages, on one reservation called the Annette Island Reserve, established in 1887, and in Alaskan cities and rural areas. Inuits and Aleuts also live in every state in the nation.

In 1980, there were 21,869 Indians, 34,144 Inuits, and 8,090 Aleuts in Alaska, over half living in Native villages and the Annette Island Reserve. Only three of these villages had more than 1,000 people—Barrow, Bethel, and Kotzebue. Seven villages had between 500 and 1,000 people. Forty villages had between fifty and one hundred people. Forty-nine villages had fewer than fifty people. Alaska Natives form sixteen percent of the total population of Alaska, the highest percentage in any state.

Each Alaska Native group has a different way of life. In the interior, a vast expanse of arctic and subarctic lands where temperatures range from 100°F in summer to 60°F below zero in winter, Athabascan Indians have adapted to the weather extremes by developing a culture based on hunting.

The Tlingit and Haida Indians live along the southeastern coast of Alaska, and the Tsimpshians live on the Annette Island Reserve in southeastern Alaska. These three groups carved the well-known totem poles. These elaborate cedar poles, reaching up to eighty feet in length, were carved and painted with figures of animals, birds, whales, and fish. By the end of the nineteenth century, very few Indians were carving poles, and by the 1930s totem poles were on the verge of disappearing, destroyed by weather and vandals. At that time, the U.S. Forest Service started a program to restore totem poles, removing many of them to protected sites. Recently, Indians have begun again to carve poles. In 1979, a pole carved by Abner Johnson, a Tlingit from Alaska, was installed on the campus of Seattle Pacific University.

Inuits live over a vast portion of the earth, in hundreds of villages in the southwest of Alaska, up Alaska's entire west coastline of over 6,600 miles, across Alaska's northern coast into Canada and Green-land, and all over the lower forty-eight. There are many dialects of the Inuit language. Among the Inuits of Alaska, two main languages, In-upiat and Yupik, are both spoken. The Inuit population is young. In

Tall totem poles of cedar wood in Southeast Alaska

Joseph C. Farber

The village of Atka, on the Aleutian Islands, is 1,000 miles from Anchorage, Alaska. The Coptic crosses of the Russian Orthodox faith, seen in the cemetery (lower left), are remnants of the days when Alaska belonged to Russia.

1980, two-thirds of the Inuits in the United States were twenty-nine years old and younger.

Before Russians arrived in what is now Alaska in the mid-1700s, most Inuits lived along the Pacific Coast and hunted sea animals. They traded seal oil, walrus and seal skins, and ivory for caribou and wolverine skins caught by Eskimos and Athabascan Indians who lived inland. Today, many Inuits continue to hunt and fish for food even though they may hold paying jobs.

In an effort to protect their language and cultural values on the international level, Inuits from Alaska, Canada, and Greenland founded in 1977 the Inuit Circumpolar Conference (ICC). Through the ICC they also hope to guard animal and bird life and the environment from industries that are polluting the Arctic.

17

One group of Alaska Natives that is not well known is the Aleuts. In 1980, the Aleut population had increased to over 14,000 from 1,700 in 1970. More than half of the Aleuts live in thirteen villages located on the Aleutian Islands; over 6,000 Aleuts live in cities and rural areas all over the lower forty-eight. These islands look like a long string that extends one thousand miles across the North Pacific Ocean. Atka, the most distant village, is about 1,000 miles from Anchorage. The names of some other Aleut villages are Akutan, False Pass, St. George, St. Paul, and Unalaska. Six of the villages had less than one hundred people. Five villages had between 150 and 500 people.

The Aleut population, like the Inuit population, is young. In 1980, almost two-thirds of the population was twenty-nine and younger.

Many scholars believe that thousands of years ago, Aleuts and Inuits had common ancestors. The two groups migrated to different places, and the Aleuts developed a remarkable culture on their rocky, mountainous, treeless islands. Sea animals provided food, clothing, and boat materials; the land provided grasses, roots, berries, and birds. Land resources also provided clothing materials and objects for ornaments.

During World War II, the United States and Japan fought for control of the Aleutian Islands. In 1942, after the Japanese captured the two westernmost Aleutian Islands for over a year, the U.S. government ordered Aleuts living near the war zone to leave their homes and be relocated to southeastern Alaska. Each person was permitted to take two suitcases of clothes; everything else had to be left behind. The Aleuts were housed in abandoned, rundown gold mines or fish canneries. Many were forced to sleep in relays because there was not enough space. About ten percent of the relocated Aleuts died from flu, measles, pneumonia, and tuberculosis. The survivors were allowed to return to their villages in 1944 and 1945, only to find their homes, possessions, and boats stolen or destroyed. The U.S. government never fully repaid the Aleuts for the theft of their furniture, boats, or fishing gear. Stolen religious objects and family treasures could of course never be replaced. A bill now being considered in Congress would provide those payments to relocated Aleuts and would also authorize the cleaning up of war debris still scattered over the islands and the repair of damaged churches.

Until recently, jobs and paper money were rare and unnecessary in Alaska Native villages. People lived on what they hunted and caught or gathered. They traded with neighboring groups for other things they needed or wanted. Today, however, Native people need cash to buy fuel for snowmobiles, for oil to heat their homes, for down jackets ordered from catalogs. Children prefer manufactured jackets to traditional handmade fur parkas. Parents need cash to buy portable stereos, radios, and televisions and to pay for electricity or batteries to run all these machines.

Today, many Alaska Natives drive cabs, fix plumbing systems, repair machines, run the post office, make baskets for craft shops in cities, work in schools, but many of these people still think of themselves as hunters first. They depend on whales, caribou, seals, ducks, and fish for part of their diet.

Over a hundred years ago, Russia and the United States changed the ancient cultures of Alaska Natives forever. By the terms of the Treaty of 1867, Russia sold Alaska to the United States. Alaska Natives argue, however, that Alaska lands have always belonged to them, long before Russians or Americans came, that Russia had no right to sell their land, and that the United States had no right to buy it.

By the 1890s, settlers from the lower forty-eight were pouring into Alaska to mine gold and copper, can salmon, and develop other resources. When Alaska became the forty-ninth state in 1959, the federal government said the state could choose about 103 million acres of public land in Alaska. When the state began selecting, Alaska Natives protested that the state was choosing lands that had always belonged to them. In 1966, the federal government halted land selections. Until 1971, Alaska Natives (through their Alaska Federation of Natives organization) and state officials struggled over ownership of Alaskan lands.

When an enormous oil deposit was discovered in Prudhoe Bay on the Arctic Coast in 1968, several major oil companies announced plans to build an 800-mile pipeline from Prudhoe Bay to Valdez. After the oil discovery, more explorers raced to the Arctic looking for oil and gas. They disturbed the privacy of ancient Inuit culture, as well as the animal life and environment that Inuits depended on. The U.S. government, at the urging of the Alaska Federation of Natives, agreed that Native land rights had to be settled before the state of Alaska or oil companies could claim any more land.

In 1971, Congress passed the Alaska Native Claims Settlement Act (ANCSA). The law gave the Natives about one-ninth of Alaskan land; in return Natives gave up all claims to the rest of Alaskan lands. The law divided Alaska into twelve regional Native business corporations, each of which includes a group of village corporations. Each corporation shared in a payment of about one billion dollars.

The names of the twelve regional corporations are Ahtna, Aleut, Arctic Slope, Bering Straits, Bristol Bay, Calista, Chugach, Cook Inlet, Doyon, Koniag, N.A.N.A., and Sealaska. A thirteenth region was set up in Seattle, Washington, for Alaska Natives who live outside of Alaska. This corporation has no land base. Today, an Alaska Native will tell you "I am enrolled in Chugach corporation" or "I am a shareholder in the Native corporation of Cook Inlet."

Regional corporations come in all sizes. The Doyon Corporation, the largest in land area, includes over thirty village corporations, encompasses over 200,000 square miles, and represents over 9,000 Alaska Natives. Doyon is one of the largest private land owners in the nation and the largest in Alaska. Koniag, the smallest corporation in land area, includes nine villages, encompasses about 7,000 square miles, and represents over 3,000 Alaska Natives.

The law provided that each person with one-quarter or more Alaska Native blood would receive one hundred shares of stock in a village corporation and one hundred shares in a regional corporation. The shares could not be sold for twenty years, until 1991. Corporation money would be invested in fish packing companies, banks, office buildings, and hotels, and each shareholder would receive dividends based on money that the corporation earned. Villages would own "surface" rights to land around the village, but the regional corporation would own everything under the land, or "mineral rights." After 1991, Alaska Natives can sell their shares in the Native corporations to anyone, including non-Natives. Many fear that when Natives are free to sell their shares non-Natives will make hard-to-resist offers and thus become shareholders in Native corporations.   \

After 1991, the state will be permitted to tax Alaska Native lands. If Natives fail to pay the state taxes on their lands, they must give them up to Alaska. If Natives sell their stock or fail to pay taxes after 1991, they will lose land. If they lose land, it may mean the end of an ancient culture that has lived for centuries in the Arctic.

ANCSA gave the Alaska Natives a land base, money, and a start at corporate business experience. But the law also contained some complicated provisions. One Alaska Native explained the situation this way. "They set us down and said 'You're a corporation, now act like one.' It would be like setting a bunch of Wall Street people down in the Arctic and saying, 'Now go catch a whale.'" People who hunted moose and seal suddenly had to deal with business statements, annual reports, and stock dividend checks.

Within the Alaska Native communities, there are heated debates over the record of ANCSA. Although the regional corporations did speed up economic growth and provide jobs, most village corporations have had financial problems. In 1985, the first village corporation filed for bankruptcy. Some corporations have used their earnings to preserve Native cultural ways. Sealaska Corporation has created com-

21

An Alaska Native regional corporation, established under the Alaska Native Claims Settlement Act of 1971, owns the Sheraton Anchorage Hotel

puterized language programs, established music and oral history libraries, and sponsored traditional celebrations. The N.A.N.A. Corporation has opened a Museum of the Arctic.

Alaska Natives are organizing in order to try to find solutions to their land problems before 1991. The ICC established the Alaska

Native Review Commission to study and prepare a report. The Commission listened to over 1,450 Natives in villages and in cities who live day to day with ANCSA. In 1985 the Commission published its report containing recommendations concerning self-government in Native villages and suggested ways of keeping Native lands under Native ownership. In 1983, thirty-six Native villages formed the United Tribes of Alaska, representing 25,000 Alaska Natives who dislike the corporate structure created by ANCSA and demand that Native lands be placed in the care of traditional tribal councils. Resolutions passed at the convention of the Alaska Federation of Natives in 1985 are meant to put additional pressure on the U.S. Congress to consider keeping Native lands in Native hands.

4

Language

There never has been one language that all Indian people living in the present-day United States speak. To believe this would be the same as believing that all people in Europe speak "European" when actually they speak French, German, Spanish, Italian, and other languages.

Experts estimate that in 1492 there were over 300 languages spoken by Native Americans in the United States and Canada. These were all separate languages. Without special learning, people who spoke one language could not understand people who spoke any of the other languages.

Related languages belong to a language family. English, French, Greek, German, Spanish, Italian, and Russian are all Indo-European languages. Even though these languages came from the same "mother," however, people who speak one of them do not automatically understand other Indo-European languages.

Indian languages also belong to families, some of which are Athabascan, Algonquian, Iroquoian, Siouan, Tanoan, and Eskimo-Aleut. Within each family, there are many offshoots or dialects of the mother language. These dialects have been spoken for thousands of years by Natives on this continent. In time they became so different that they evolved into languages of their own, having only a slight similarity to the original language. For example, the language spoken by the Cahuilla of southern California is related to that spoken by the Paiutes of Nevada. Both languages are in the Utaztecan family. Navajos of Arizona speak a language related to the Tlingits of Alaska; both languages are in the Athabascan family.

Indian languages have contributed to English and to many other languages around the world. Native Americans had their own names for rivers, trees, mountains, mammals, plants, and towns and villages. Some cities, towns, and states in this country still have these ancient names, although the pronunciation may have changed over the years. Three states have their original names. Idaho is a Shoshone word meaning "salmon eaters." Kansas is a Sioux word that means "south wind." Minnesota is probably a Sioux word that means "milky or clouded water." Twenty-two other states have names of Indian origin.

ALABAMA—Creek word, true meaning unknown.

ALASKA—Aleut or Inuit word, meaning "great lands" or a designation for Native lands.

ARIZONA—Spanish version of Papago and Pima word, meaning "little spring place" or "site of the small springs" (lack of water).

ARKANSAS—French version of a Sioux word for Kansas or "south wind people."

CONNECTICUT—Mohegan word, meaning "long river place" or "river whose waters are driven in waves by tides or winds"; appears to be taken from the word *Quonoktacut*.

ILLINOIS—French version of the Indian word *Illini*, meaning "man" or "warrior."

IOWA—Sioux tribal name, meaning "sleepy ones" or "one who puts to sleep."

KENTUCKY—Wyandot-Iroquoian word; meaning "plain" or "meadow land."

MASSACHUSETTS—Algonquian word, meaning "large hill place." The state is named after the Massachusetts Indians.

MICHIGAN—Chippewa word, meaning "big lake" or "clearing."

MISSISSIPPI—Chippewa or Choctaw word, meaning "large river."

MISSOURI—tribe unknown, meaning "canoe carrier" or "muddy water."

NEBRASKA—Omaha word, meaning "broad water."

NEW MEXICO—Aztec word, meaning taken from the Aztec god, Mexitli.

NORTH AND SOUTH DAKOTA—Sioux words, meaning "friend" or "allies."

OHIO—Iroquois word, meaning "beautiful river."

OKLAHOMA—Choctaw word, meaning "red people."

TEXAS—Spanish version of Caddo word, meaning "friend" or "allies."

UTAH—Apache word, meaning "one that is higher up." This refers to Ute Indians who lived higher up in mountain country than the Apache of the region.

WISCONSIN—Chippewa word, meaning "grassy place" or "wild rushing channel."

WYOMING—Lenni Lenape word, meaning "large prairie place" or "mountains with valleys alternating."

Indian languages have contributed thousands of words to the English language, including raccoon, coyote, squash, tapioca, tobacco, succotash, barbecue, hurricane, hammock, canoe, moccasin, totem, and powwow.

Over hundreds of years, Indian names for places, animals, and plants have been replaced by names chosen by English, Spanish, French, German, and other Europeans who settled all over the nation. For example, the Spanish who settled in California gave Spanish names to places that originally had Indian names. Southern California Indians called Agua Caliente (hot water in Spanish) *Se-chi.* They called Cabezon *Pal-te-nai* and Santa Rosa *We-Wut-Now-Hut.*

Traditional Indian languages were not written down. Language and all knowledge were stored in people's memories and passed on to the next generation through legends, stories, and myths. Many tribes used picture writing, drawing on birchbark and animal skins and carving pictures on wood and stone to record important events within the tribe. The pictures did not represent language sounds, however.

In 1821, Sequoyah, a Cherokee, invented an alphabet of symbols that represented sounds in the Cherokee language. This alphabet of over eighty symbols permitted Cherokees to write their language on paper. In a little over a year they were able to read and write their own language. The U.S. Postal Service honored Sequoyah's achievement by releasing a 19¢ Sequoyah postage stamp in December 1980. Since 1828 a few other Indian languages have been recorded on paper as well, but for the most part Indian languages have been handed down by word of mouth from one generation to the next.

Around 150 to 200 Indian and Alaska Native languages continue to be spoken in communities today. Some of these languages are stronger than others because there are more speakers who know them. Navajo, Lakota, and Yupik (Eskimo) are widely spoken.

Some Indian people speak a Native language as their first language. For example, the Coushatta language is spoken in all homes on the Louisiana reservation. Coushatta children do not speak English until they enter Coushatta preschool or public school. Many Navajo children who live on the reservation do not speak English until they attend school. Choctaw is spoken as the first language in over ninety percent of the Mississippi Choctaw homes.

These Indian languages are as different from one another as English is from Chinese. The Hopis cannot understand the Tlingit language any more than the Spanish can understand the Tibetan language.

Many Indian languages were lost in the late 1800s and early 1900s when Indian children were forced to go to boarding schools run by the U.S. government. In some of these schools, children were forbidden to speak their own languages and were punished when they did so.

Paul Conklin

A few words of Navajo, an Athabascan language, written by a school child

This ban unfortunately was so effective that over 150 Native American languages died off because people stopped speaking them. Since most of these languages were never written down, there is no way to recover them.

At a Native American language conference held in 1985, ways of preserving traditional languages were discussed. It was reported that Indian people in Washington State have all but lost their Native languages, that only about eight members of the Gros Ventre Tribe in Montana still speak the tribal language, and that among the Pomos in northern California, there are some five elders who speak the language. In the late 1960s, the last Chitimacha Indian in Louisiana who spoke the language died. On the other hand, about eighty percent of Crow children who enter school know their own language.

Throughout the nation, Indians are trying to preserve languages before they slip away. They are videotaping and tape recording elders speaking their languages. Indian-controlled schools and community colleges and public schools serving Indian communities have bilingual programs. Children learn how to read and write and do their school lessons in their own language as well as in English. Bilingual programs use schools materials that have tribal viewpoints so children learn to respect their tribal ways. Many adults also take reading and writing courses in Indian languages.

It is difficult for non-Indians to learn Indian languages. Some sounds in Indian languages do not exist in English. In about one-third of Indian languages, the sounds of k, p, or t are pronounced while holding the breath or almost choking. There are some whispered consonants and vowels, unpronounced consonants, hisses, and sharp exhalings. Some Indian languages have tones. Word meanings change with the high and low sounds of vowels. Many words in Indian languages begin with "ts" or "tl." These are difficult letter combinations for English speakers. Many words are so long that they are more like phrases. One linguist recorded a Southern Paiute word, *wii-to-kuchum-punku-rugani-yugwi-va-ntu-mlu,* which means they who are going to sit and cut up with a knife a black cow buffalo. It is difficult to translate from an Indian language to English because it is not always possible to capture the original meanings of the words.

Indian grammars are complicated and different from English. In the Hopi language, for example, verbs have no tense.

It is possible but extremely difficult for non-Indians to learn an Indian language. First, there are few places where one can take a course in Lakota, Navajo, or Yupik. Indian languages are taught in Indian-controlled schools like Rough Rock Demonstration School in Arizona or in Indian community colleges like Sinte Gleska Community College in South Dakota or Navajo Community College in Arizona.

Non-Indians can buy dictionaries of Indian languages or school materials printed in English and an Indian language. The Navajo Curriculum Center publishes many learning materials in the Navajo and English languages.

Some linguists are working with Indian people to produce dictionaries of unwritten Indian languages. One professor of linguistics has been working with the Gros Ventres to complete a dictionary of their language before the last speaker dies. He asks Gros Ventres to repeat a word over and over until he has written its pronunciation in an international system of phonetic symbols. The Coushattas are also working on a tribal dictionary.

About a dozen tribes have their own radio stations that broadcast some programs in Indian languages. On the Rosebud Sioux Reservation in South Dakota, radio station KINI (meaning new beginning), starts each day with the Sioux National Anthem and broadcasts news in Lakota and in English.

5

Daily Lives

Indians and Alaska Natives today live, eat, and dress differently from
their ancestors. Long ago, Wichita Indians lived in grass houses,
Lakotas (Sioux) in buffalo-hide tipis, Mohawks in bark-covered longhouses, Seminoles in thatch-and-pine chickees, Navajos in stone
hogans, Pawnees in earth lodges, and Zunis in adobe and stone rooms
built against one another to form a village that looks like apartments.

Some of these traditional house styles survive today. People either
live in them or use them for some other purpose. Today, Indians use
new materials to build some of the traditionally shaped houses. Many
Navajo families in Arizona or New Mexico continue to live in hogans,
which are circular or six-or-more-sided dwellings made of logs or
stones and earth or cement. In New Mexico, Taos Pueblo families still
live in apartment-like stone houses called pueblos. In the other
pueblos in New Mexico, people use the few remaining multi-storied
houses for worship and other activities.

Hundreds of years ago, the Iroquois nations (Cayugas, Mohawks,
Oneidas, Onondagas, Senecas, and Tuscaroras) in present-day New
York lived in rectangular longhouses that were fifty to one hundred-
fifty feet long, fifteen to twenty feet high, and about twenty feet wide.
These long, large houses accommodated as many as a dozen related
families. Today longhouses are not used for everyday living but for

31

Nelson Navarro, United Methodist Board of Global Ministries

A Navajo hogan near Shiprock, New Mexico

Joseph C. Farber

A Taos Pueblo in New Mexico

Joseph C. Farber

Miccosukee chickees in southern Florida

special events: ceremonies, social gatherings and dances, marriages and burial services, and meetings.

Miccosukees of southern Florida used to live in chickees, open-sided dwellings that were suited for hot, humid climates. Today, most Miccosukees live in frame or cement-block houses. Some families build a chickee and use it for sewing or other purposes. They are cool places to work.

Today, Indians do not live in tipis. Over a hundred years ago, however, some groups—including the Sioux, Crow, Blackfeet, and Cheyenne—did live in these triangular-shaped dwellings. They lived on the Great Plains, which include the present-day states of North and South Dakota, Montana, Oklahoma, Kansas, Nebraska, Idaho, Wyoming, Colorado, and parts of Utah and Texas. Although Indians stopped living in tipis by the 1930s, modern Indians all over the country pitch tipis made of canvas at powwows, ceremonials, and even in amusement parks. Tipis have become a symbol of Indian-style houses.

33

Indians are a deeply religious people. Hundreds of years ago, before contact with Europeans, they considered their homes spiritual places. Some still do. The Navajos still treat their hogans as sacred places. Before a hogan is used by a family, the head of the household blesses it, turning clockwise, sprinkling ceremonial corn pollen on the four main house posts. People bless hogans with at least two prayers and four songs. The hogan's one door faces east so that powerful, early morning light may enter the house. People also perform sacred healing ceremonies in hogans.

Today, many Indians on reservations and in cities live in modern houses, low-rent housing, apartments, mobile homes, and subdivisions.

Dozens of houses on reservations are old and run down. Indians simply do not have money to repair them. Some Indian people live in log cabins or one-room cinder-block houses that are drafty and do not have indoor bathrooms, running water, phones, or electricity. Others live in cramped trailers. In 1984, the Bureau of Indian Affairs reported that some 38,000 Indian homes did not have adequate safe water and indoor plumbing. Many Indian families depend on water hauled from ditches, hand wells, and melted snow. Some Indians in cities frequently live in apartments and houses that are drafty, cramped, cold, and unsanitary.

Today, tribes as well as the federal government recognize that housing is a severe problem for Indians. They are trying to provide decent, safe, and sanitary houses on Indian reservations, but there are obstacles. Many agencies like the Bureau of Indian Affairs, the Indian Health Service, the Army Corps of Engineers, the National Park Service, the Department of Transportation, and the Department of Housing and Urban Development require Indian people to fill out numerous forms before building a house. New houses must not be built over archaeological sites. New house owners must get approval for new roads. Finally, Indians with low incomes must figure out ways to get

Joseph C. Farber

Many Indians do not have indoor running water and must haul water from wherever they can find it

the money to pay for their houses. Even Indians who have decent incomes find it difficult to get loans from banks.

Today, Native Americans usually buy their food in supermarkets or grocery stores like most people do, but some still rely on traditional methods of getting and preparing foods. For example, Chippewas who live on Wisconsin reservations participate in the yearly harvest of wild rice. Men move canoes through rice fields while women knock stalks with ricing sticks causing ripened wild rice grains to drop into the canoes. Chippewas do not allow machines to harvest the rice from the stalk, but some use machines to clean, thresh, and winnow. In the Southwest, Hopi mothers and grandmothers teach young girls how to grind corn on stone slabs passed down from generation to generation. The young women prepare a special thin bread called *piki* with blue cornmeal and make the ceremonial *chukuviki*, small pointed loaves steamed in corn-husk wrappers. In the Northwest, Indians catch salmon and often prepare them traditionally in smokehouses.

Many Indian people still gather wild berries, roots, nuts, and herbs on their reservations. In South Dakota and North Dakota, people gather wild chokecherries and dry and pound them to make a pudding served with meat dishes.

Tribal people living in the days before supermarkets never took food for granted. They respected the sun, rain, and earth that provided nourishment and showed their respect to Mother Earth in prayers,

Chippewas in Minnesota and Wisconsin harvest rice the traditional way, with ric-ing sticks from aluminum canoes

Joseph C. Farber

Pena Bonita

Corn growing on the Mescalero (Apache) Reservation in New Mexico

songs, ceremonies, and dances of thankfulness. Today, Indian people continue this tradition of showing appreciation for food in ceremonies. In New York State, the Iroquois nations hold a maple festival, or tree thanksgiving ceremony, at the beginning of March. People dance to honor the spirit that caused the sap to rise again. In summer, the Iroquois have a Green Corn Ceremony to give thanks for the corn crop. In Arizona and New Mexico, many Pueblo people honor the sacred nature of food through daily prayer. In the Northwest, the people hold a first salmon ceremony to give thanks for the life-preserving fish. After the first salmon is caught, people carry it to the village and prepare it in special ways. The next morning, people say prayers, and each person receives a piece of the fish.

At powwows and other social gatherings, Indian people prepare feasts of traditional food. One popular food is frybread, dough patted out into plate-sized rounds, deep-fried until golden brown, and some-

37

times sprinkled with powdered sugar. In old times, tribal people believed food was for everyone so they always shared their food with people who had less. The sharing continues today.

American Indian cooking is nutritious, delicious, and varied. Native people continue to make traditional dishes. Recipes for many of these dishes may be found in books about American Indian cooking. Now anyone can prepare and sample Zuni green chili stew or Choctaw shrimp stew, Muckleshoot raspberry sauce, Iroquois soup, Navajo griddle cake, Apache ash bread, or Havasupai squash-blossom pudding.

Nowadays, Native American people often wear manufactured jeans, shirts, skirts, sweaters, and sneakers most of the time and save their traditional clothes for dances, powwows, ceremonies, and other special

Joseph C. Farber

A Miccosukee man wears a patchwork jacket over his store-bought clothes

occasions. Several tribal groups, however, wear distinctive traditional clothing every day. Around the beginning of this century, Miccosukee women traded alligator hides, furs, and exotic feathers for hand-cranked sewing machines, cloth, and thread. They developed a patch-work technique by sewing one piece of cloth to another to form patterns. They used these patchwork designs as decoration for clothing. Today, Miccosukee women, men, and children, of Florida, wear vests, dresses, shirts, skirts, and jackets decorated with rows of colorful geometric patchwork designs. Miccosukee men like to wear their jackets over manufactured everyday clothing. These clothes have become an identifying mark of the Florida Indian.

Sewing without patterns or drawings, Miccosukee women have developed patchwork into an impressive art form. Every year, during the Miccosukee Art Festival, contemporary patchwork styles are displayed in a fashion show. The women continue to invent new ways to use patchwork.

For more than one hundred years, Navajo women have worn fitted velvet and velveteen blouses with full, long cotton skirts. They saw this style of dress on non-Indian women in the late 1860s and created their own version. Most Apache women in Arizona, New Mexico, and Oklahoma have worn full, long skirts with loose blouses, both decorated with bands of trim, since the late 1800s. Women from the Papago, Yaqui, and Maricopa Tribes in Arizona also wear loose-fitting, two-piece outfits.

Pueblo women wear mantas, handwoven belted dresses wrapped under the left arm and fastened at the right shoulder. The dark blue, black, or brown cloth is decorated at the borders with embroidery. Pueblo men wear woven kilts wrapped around their waists. The white kilts have designs in red, green, and black that symbolize rain, clouds, and growing crops. These designs have been embroidered on men's shirts as well.

Some older Pueblo, Navajo, and Apache women wear traditional

clothing every day. Most younger women wear it only for special ceremonies.

Indian women in the Great Lakes area have developed a unique and
complicated method of adding ribbons to shirts. Now Native American men and women throughout the United States wear modern ribbon shirts called *bethaqual.* They wear them at dances and festivals and
powwows. Many young Indians wear the shirts all the time as a symbol

Elizabeth Lenell

LuAnn Jamieson, member of the Tonawanda Seneca Nation, models a gown cre-
ated by Kathy Dalrymple, Western Cherokee fashion designer

of pride in their Indian ancestry. At powwows, Indian people sell the ribbon shirts to the public.

Indians of the Pacific Northwest wear "button blankets" at ceremonies. These are dark blankets on which red flannel and as many as 1,000 or more pearl buttons are sewn in the shape of animals. Usually button blankets depict the thunderbird, eagle, whale, or other animal that is the symbol of a certain clan a person belongs to.

American Indians and Inuits have influenced the way other Americans dress. Moccasin-type shoes, parkas, headbands, and ponchos have been adapted from Indian styles. Several Native American dress designers are creating contemporary clothes and accessories with American Indian designs done with applique, beads, shells, and ribbons. In 1985 these fashion designers from all parts of the United States gathered for the first time in Denver, Colorado, to show their evening-wear creations that adapted traditional Indian designs to contemporary fabrics and styles.

6

Religious Ways

Before Europeans came to North America, the religious life of Native Americans was not separate from their daily lives. Religion was not a Friday night, Saturday morning, or Sunday morning activity. It surrounded Indian people every day. Some part of almost every action was likely to be religious. In fact, Indian languages did not even have a word for religion because it was not separate from daily life.

Indian religions are based on nature and the supernatural, unseen powers. Indians believe that the power of the supernatural is found in everything. Therefore they respect plants, mammals, birds, fish, minerals—everything created by the supernatural. Indians feel that all living things in the universe depend on one another and are interrelated. Their traditions, sacred practices, dances, songs, legends, designs on everyday objects, and ceremonies are patterned on the natural world.

In traditional Native American religions, a relationship with the supernatural is maintained through worship in ceremonial dances, worship at sacred natural sites, and the use of sacred natural objects. Worship is the way Native people show respect for the supernatural, ask for help, and give thanks. There are many kinds of prayers. Before people plant corn or kill an animal, for example, they pray in order to make themselves aware of what they are doing to themselves, to their community, and to nature.

Religious Ways

Since tribes are different from one another, religious traditions differ from tribe to tribe. All tribes have a name in their languages for the unseen supernatural power. The Cheyennes call it *Maheo*, the Mohawks *Orenda*, the Lakota (Sioux) *Wakan Tanka*, the Shoshones *Pokunt*, the Micmac *Manitoo*.

Each tribe has its own sacred stories that explain the universe and the unknown just as there are explanations about these things in the Bible. Each tribe has its own ceremonies to perform according to instructions given in the sacred stories. These ceremonies are performed in order to create favorable relationships with spirit beings.

Each ceremony is performed for a specific reason. There are ceremonies that mark the important changes in an individual's life—birth, naming, renaming, coming-of-age, marriage, and death. Ceremonies mark important times of the year, like the winter and summer solstices (when the sun is at its greatest distance from the equator) and the spring and fall equinox (when day and night all over the earth are of equal length). There are ceremonies for healing sickness, renewing relationships with spiritual beings, initiating people into spiritual societies, assuring success in hunting and planting and growing crops, bringing rain or guarding against drought, giving thanks for harvests of food, requesting protection from cold and winds. There are acorn, strawberry, and bean festivals. There are festivals for green corn, young corn, yellow, white, red, blue, and black corn.

Each ceremony is performed at a particular time and place for a set number of days. People who participate in or observe ceremonies have to prepare. For some ceremonies, people purify themselves in sweat lodges, small, domelike structures made of saplings and covered with hides or canvas. Inside, steam is produced by pouring cold water over hot stones. People sit in steam to purify their bodies for the ceremony. They also use sweat to treat sickness. The sweat lodge is a place to teach the young about the tribe's traditions.

Indians gather natural objects and sometimes put on special clothes for ceremonies. There are instructions about who may attend the ceremony, how to arrive, how to behave before it starts, how to behave after the ceremony ends, how to leave. People whose behavior might hurt the ceremony are not allowed to take part.

Years ago, these ceremonies were as important to Native peoples as eating and sleeping. The whole community participated in a drama that was exciting and far from ordinary everyday life, ceremonies that appealed to the imagination and emotions. There were songs, dances, special foods, decorated clothes and objects, masks, makeup, and music.

Many tribes continue to perform some of their ancient ceremonies in the traditional way. For example, the Hopis of Arizona perform nine-centuries-old ceremonies throughout the year, based on their own calendar, each lasting from nine to sixteen days. Each Hopi village has a plaza where ceremonies take place. During late spring and early summer months, at least one Hopi village has a ceremony in its plaza every weekend. Some portions of each ceremony are held in *kivas,* sacred circular, underground structures. Only certain people are allowed to witness these rituals. Visitors are allowed to attend some of the ceremonial dances, but they must dress correctly and keep still during the sacred dancing. Even other Indians are sometimes excluded from some portions of the ceremonies. Many Hopis prefer not to share information about their ceremonies with those who do not speak their language, share their culture, or understand the meaning and sacredness of the dances. They believe sharing this information will ruin the ceremonies and weaken the Hopi religion.

Many other tribes also keep much of their sacred ways secret. In 1984, a newspaper, the *Santa Fe New Mexican,* printed photos of a Santo Domingo Pueblo religious ceremony taken from a low-flying plane. The editors did not have permission to photograph this secret ceremony, and the Pueblo sued the paper for invading its privacy. Eventually, officials of the newspaper apologized, agreed to be more sensitive to Indian culture, and agreed to give the tribe college scholarships for Pueblo students.

Nearly all religious groups have places that are special in their religion. In traditional Indian religions these places are outdoors, and many Indians continue to believe that certain areas are holy because religious events occurred there, because they contain special natural products or burial grounds, or because they are the dwelling places of spiritual beings or sites considered perfect for communicating with spiritual beings. Mounds, caves, mountains, streams, and hot springs may be holy places. Today these places may be on land owned by Indians or by non-Indians.

The Northern Cheyennes of Montana consider Bear Butte, near Sturgis, South Dakota, a sacred place. Their religious history includes the belief that the first Cheyenne people were born there. Every year many people from the tribe travel to Bear Butte to fast, to pray for themselves and their families and for spiritual guidance. Today Bear Butte is in a South Dakota state park. At times, non-Indian people in the park disturb Cheyennes who are praying there.

Tribes have religious laws that spell out what ceremonies may take place at sacred sites, who may attend them, and what will happen to an individual, group, or tribe if the laws are broken.

Many sacred grounds have been destroyed, leaving Indians no way to worship at their sites. In Arizona, authorities flooded a sacred site of the Navajos to create Lake Powell. According to Navajo belief, the deities were drowned by this action. Representatives of the federal government, ignoring Indian protests, have argued that the Arizona flooding brought benefits to a large population.

Coso Hot Springs, in California, is important to the religious life of the Paiute and Shoshone Indians as a sacred place for spiritual and physical renewal and curing. The U.S. Navy acquired the springs after World War II for the storage of ammunition and, for reasons of national security, would not permit Indians to visit. After Congress

45

This is a place sacred to the Northern Cheyennes. In the foreground is a buffalo skull filled with sweet grass, which is used in religious ceremonies.

This is the entrance to a Mandan earth lodge, a sacred site in North Dakota used for ceremonies.

passed legislation in 1978 protecting Indian religious practices, the Navy agreed to allow certain tribal religious activities at Coso Hot Springs.

In central California, the Chumash people have long considered Santa Lucia Peak, located in a United States forest, a sacred site. The Chumash used to bury sacred objects at the top of the peak to help the dead on their journey to the spirit world. The Forest Service has denied requests from Chumash people to go to the Peak.

Sometimes, sacred grounds are disturbed. Construction projects, farming, and archaeological digs accidentally uncover burial sites. At times, farmers, archaeologists, or construction workers who discover Indian bones and objects buried with the dead have taken these remains and kept them, sold them, or donated them to museums.

In recent decades, Congress returned to the people of Taos Pueblo their sacred Blue Lake, an area located high in the Sangre de Christo Mountains of northern New Mexico. The lake and the land around it had been taken from the Pueblo and made a part of Carson National Forest. In 1974, Mount Adams in Washington State was returned to the Yakima Nation. In 1984, Congress returned a sacred site in Arizona to the New Mexico Pueblo of Zuni.

People who practice traditional Indian religions use natural objects in ceremonies. In 1978, an Otoe Indian of Oklahoma explained to a U.S. Senate committee:

> In trying to express their thankful appreciation for life in this world, [Indians] developed religious ceremonies to glorify the Creator . . . they used various things in their ceremonies such as the feathers of various birds and their parts, skins and pelts of the animals and their parts, various vegetation and different kinds of herbs they found that had healing properties, different kinds of woods, rocks, and things of the water such as sea shells, pelts of the seal, and tusks of the walrus . . .

People do not worship these objects. They wear, hold, eat, carry, bury, or simply look at them. Drums, arrows, masks, pipes, medicine bundles, and other objects made from natural materials are used in Native American religious ceremonies. Rocks, roots, berries, gourds, leaves, shells, turquoise, and other things are used to purify, heal, or help people seek visions.

Indian religious leaders often travel to traditional places to gather materials necessary for ceremonies only to find they are turned away and cannot gather what they need. The materials may be on land owned by the U.S. Park Service or the U.S. Forest Service. U.S. laws protect certain fish, wildlife, and plants because there are so few of them left. These conservation laws, too, have prevented some Indians from getting the natural objects they need for ceremonies and worship.

Indians have used parts of birds, fish, mammals, plants, and minerals in religious ceremonies for centuries without endangering any forms of life. It was only after Europeans had settled in the United States that large numbers of mammals and fish were killed for food. During the late nineteenth century, bison were almost made extinct. Federal dams built in the 1940s and 1950s reduced seventy-five percent of the wildlife and plants on Sioux reservations in South Dakota and flooded many sacred sites.

In 1978, Congress passed the American Indian Religious Freedom Act to protect the rights of American Indians and Alaska Natives to believe, express, and exercise their traditional religions. This act protects the right of Indians to use sacred areas and to obtain and use natural objects necessary for worship. Federal officials in various agencies are trying to work with Indians to protect their religious rights while at the same time protecting endangered plants and animals.

The government has not always been so understanding. During the late nineteenth century and early twentieth century, the federal government punished Indian people for practicing their traditional religions. In 1892, the Commissioner of Indian Affairs declared:

Any Indian who shall engage in the sun dance . . . or any similar feast . . . shall be deemed guilty of an offense, and upon conviction thereof shall be punished for the first offense by the withholding of his rations . . . or by imprisonment for not exceeding ten days.

He also ordered that

Any Indian who shall engage in the practices of so-called medicine men . . . shall be deemed guilty of an offense, and upon conviction . . . for the first offense shall be imprisoned for not less than ten nor more than thirty days.

The U.S. government sent missionaries to reservations to convert tribal members to Christianity. Baptist, Roman Catholic, Presbyterian, Episcopalian, and other missionaries worked among tribes trying to replace tribal religions with Christianity.

In some Indian groups, traditional religion survived and remained strong. On other reservations, tribal religious leaders blended ancient Indian teachings with the newer Christian beliefs. In still other tribal groups members abandoned their Indian sacred ways and became practicing Christians and even Christian missionaries.

Today, traditional religions are stronger in some Indian groups than in others. Sometimes it is only the elders who practice the sacred ways everyday. Some Indian people do not know their tribe's religious beliefs. On the other hand, many young Indians, both on reservations and in cities, are interested in learning their traditional religions and spirituality.

In some tribes, members consider themselves Christian but also perform traditional Indian sacred ways. Some Sioux worship Christ and also pray to *Wakan Tanka,* the Great Spirit. It is not unusual for a Choctaw elder to be both a traditional religious leader and a deacon in his local Christian church. Many Indians pray in churches and go to healing ceremonies immediately afterwards. These Indian people view the Indian and Christian traditions as of separate but equal value. They were not brought up to give all their faith and support to one denomination, so they are able to support two or even three different religions at the same time.

On many reservations, traditional Indian religion has combined with a Christian religion to create a new way to worship. The Yaquis of Arizona have combined ancient Yaqui sacred ways with Catholic practices. The Choctaws of Mississippi have combined their older re-

50

ligion with Protestantism and created a new sacred way. At Christmas, Acoma Indians of New Mexico dance and chant to fiddles and drums for four days and four nights, in headdresses and mammal skins. They celebrate the Christian holiday by mixing Christian and Acoma Pueblo religious practices.

Some Indians have created new religions that attract members from many tribes. The Native American Church, which uses Christian rituals, has followers in Oklahoma and other parts of the nation.

Today, Indians are not surrounded by religion as they were before Europeans came. A great deal of Indian life is now concerned with nonsacred, or secular, things. Just like everyone else, Indians worry about jobs, having enough food, and leaky roofs. Nowadays, most Indians separate their lives into the sacred and the secular. They go to work or school (secular) and to ceremonies (sacred). Indian women prepare a special drink from cornmeal (sacred), but they buy their canned milk and maybe the cornmeal, too, at stores (secular). These divisions did not exist in the lives of Native Americans before contact with European ways.

7

Dance and Music

Before Europeans came to America, Indian peoples worshiped by dancing and many still do. They feel closer to and in harmony with all living things and unseen forces of the universe. Not every Indian could weave a basket or create a clay jar, but nearly every person could dance and sing songs. Dance is still very important in some Indian groups. People take part in ceremonial dances to express themselves in much the same way people go to church to pray. A member of the San Juan Pueblo has said, "If there is no one here to carry on the dances, our whole society might fall apart." Many Indians continue to dance to keep old ways alive, to connect themselves to the past, and to pray.

Indians dance for many reasons: to heal the sick, to mourn, to bring rain for crops, to give thanks, to bring a good harvest, to protect themselves from danger, to help in hunting, to gain strength, to welcome the arrival of friends, and to honor their departure.

Dancers practice for years to perfect skills for certain dances. They rehearse each step, motion, gesture, and beat. Indians feel the finished presentation has to be as near perfect as possible to earn the attention of the spirit power to whom the dance is directed. Some dance steps are simple, others complicated. Dancers usually move in a circle clockwise, as the sun moves.

Most Indian groups have sacred clowns who perform pranks, talking and moving backwards. These clowns make people laugh, but they really have important messages. They make fun of bad behavior, make people forget their sadness or sickness for a little while, make them think about everyday things in a new way, and make them look at problems in a new way.

Each tribe has its own steps, clothing, decorated objects, and traditional movements. The Apaches have a Mountain Spirit Dance that welcomes young Apache girls into womanhood. They also perform this dance during difficult times when they seek guidance and healing from the mountain spirits. The dance was performed in 1965 for President Lyndon Johnson, the first time in history that Indian dancers had performed at the White House. In this dance and in other tribal dances, Indians transform themselves into animals. The Utes honor bears in their dances. The Pueblos and most other tribes have an Eagle Dance. Some Inuit groups honor wolves. There are even dances that honor butterflies.

The Pueblo groups of New Mexico still continue to perform centuries-old dances that follow the seasons: harvest dances in the fall to thank Mother Earth for crops and rain, animal and hunting dances in the winter, dances for planting new crops in the spring, and in the summer dances that call for rain to help crops grow.

The times of some dances change from year to year while others are held on the same date every year. Today some pueblos have their dances on weekends so that people who work off the reservation can get home for the dancing.

Pueblo dances are complex. There are specific steps for certain dances, special formations for groups as a whole, certain ways to turn and move together, special ways to interact with the music, ways to move the upper body, legs, and arms, times to come and go to the dance, things to do before and after the dance, special clothing to wear, and special decorated objects to carry—all depending on the dance and the pueblo.

Joseph C. Farber

An Eagle Dance in the Southwest

Many dances tell stories and legends and history. For example, the San Ildefonso, Tesuque, and Taos Pueblo Indians have Comanche Dances that tell, in dance form, of the coming of Comanches from the Plains to the Pueblo Indian country.

People sometimes chant while they dance. They carry gourd rattles or wear bells, turtle shells, deer hooves, bones, and bits of stones tied below their knees. All these objects make sounds as the dancers move.

The color, movements, sounds, clothing, and decorations of traditional Indian dance inspire many Indian artists today. Painters depict traditional Indian dancers. Sculptors create dancers in metal and stone. Poets use words to create images of the dancers.

Dance and Music

Many traditional dances and songs no longer exist. Some are re-membered only by the elders of the tribes. Other songs and dances were stopped by the government in the late nineteenth century and now are no longer performed because people have forgotten them. Some Indian youngsters today do not learn or perform the dances or songs since they do not feel the need for them in their daily lives, but other young Indians and Inuits have continued to learn and worship through their tribal dances.

Indian people also worship through singing. Indians sing songs from the beginning of life to the end, songs for good health, for the growth of crops, for good hunting. They sing children to sleep, to honor peo-ple, to heal people, to ensure peace, and just for fun. Music, like religion, once was part of daily life and continues to be important to many Indians today.

Music differs from tribe to tribe. Some music has sounds but no words; other music has both sounds and words. At times, drums, rat-tles, or flutes accompany songs. Some music has no instrumental ac-companiment. Some tribes sing songs exactly as they were sung hundreds of years ago; others compose new songs every year but repeat the old songs as well. Each tribe has its own social, ceremonial, and religious songs.

Outsiders can listen to tribal songs sung at powwows or at cere-monies like flag raisings, memorial services, or on special occasions when someone is being honored. Outsiders rarely hear religious songs, however; only initiated people hear these songs at secret rites.

Some songs come to people in visions or dreams and are thus the personal property of individual Indians. These kinds of songs are highly prized by Indians.

Almost all songs are accompanied by a drum. There are small drums that fit into the hand and drums large enough for several singers to sit around. They are made from different materials: double-headed and single-headed drums covered with animal skins, basket drums, clay drums, wooden drums, metal drums, and some drums that contain water. There are square, triangular, and round drums. All these drums have different "voices," depending on the sizes and materials of the beaters and the amount of hollow air space inside the drums. Some drums are used only for religious songs, some are used only for social occasions, and some are used for both.

The Plains tribes have recorded many of their songs. The Pueblos have recorded some songs but prefer to guard them, especially those used in sacred ceremonies. Canyon Records in Phoenix, Arizona, has been recording Indian music since 1952 and now has more than 400 records and tapes of traditional songs and chants of singers and groups from all over the United States. Some of these songs have all but disappeared with the death of elderly Indians. Among those recorded are Flathead stick game songs, Sioux rabbit songs, Chippewa flag songs, Winnebago green corn dance songs, Caddo turkey dance songs, Apache thunder songs, Navajo goat songs, Hopi butterfly dance songs, Pima rainbow songs, Inuit hunting songs, and Nootka canoe paddling songs.

For almost twenty years, the Indian House of Taos, New Mexico, has been recording the music of some of the finest traditional Indian musicians and composers of the United States. The Library of Congress in Washington, D.C., and Folkways Records in New York City also have collections of traditional music.

8

Sacred Healers

In every American Indian and Alaska Native village, there are people who are responsible for special, sometimes secret, knowledge and practices. They know sacred stories that contain information about where the tribal people came from, explain unseen powers, tell how everything in the universe was created, and teach proper behavior. These stories contain knowledge about how to survive in the world by performing ceremonies, prayers, dances, and using special herbs. The people who know these stories are the tribes' libraries. Information is stored and preserved not in books but in their memories. This oral tradition once was the way Indian people maintained the sacred ways and customs of the tribes. Sacred people also have the responsibility of passing this knowledge on to younger generations.

Since it is impossible for one person to know everything about the sacred ways of his or her culture, knowledge is vested in many people. Certain people diagnose illness; others know how to use herbs that cure people of illness. There are people who know one or more healing ceremonies and people who know songs that help bring about success in hunting, or bring rain, or help the growing crops.

Some people learn when they are very young that they have a gift for sacred knowledge. Something extraordinary may happen to them. They may have recovered from a serious illness or hear voices at night or have a strange dream or vision filled with fragments of sacred ways. When this happens they must become sacred people whether they want to or not. They feel they have been chosen. Once people are aware that they have special gifts, they usually ask an experienced sacred person for guidance and advice. These experienced people teach and train those who wish to become sacred. It takes years of difficult work to learn the special knowledge.

Sometimes the inexperienced person has to seek knowledge through dreams or vision quests, usually alone and isolated for two to four days. If successful, they encounter spirit beings that give them power and direction in life. Experienced medicine men and women watch over a person preparing for a vision quest and choose the sacred ground where a person might receive a guiding vision to follow during life. After a successful quest, they explain the meanings of the experience to those who acquire supernatural guidance.

After a successful spiritual encounter, these special people are considered religious leaders and spend the rest of their lives learning and practicing sacred ways. Although this is a highly regarded occupation, such people also have jobs, farm, and do housework and whatever else is necessary for living.

These shamans or medicine men or women, as they have come to be called, use their sacred knowledge to help keep people healthy. To sacred healers, being ill means being out of tune with nature and the supernatural. Sacred healing, then, is much more than treating a disease with medicine or healing a broken bone. Sacred healers believe that a person is made up of body, mind, and spirit and that all must be in balance with that person's community and natural world. Shamans try to rebalance elements in ill bodies so that patients can heal themselves and return to a proper balance with nature and the supernatural.

Some Indian people who are ill go to shamans or medicine men or women to find out what has caused their illness. One sacred person diagnoses the cause of the illness or the imbalance. Then another medicine man or woman prescribes a cure. The patient must follow strict rules before and after healing ceremonies. In ceremonies, healers use fasting, sweating, cold applications, herbs, and chants to cure people. Medicine men or women are paid for their services with gifts or money depending on how long or complicated the ceremony was.

Among the Navajos today, there are various kinds of sacred healers. Some medicine men know how to choose the proper healing ceremony or "sing" for an ill person. Some Navajo medicine men know a great deal about herbs and plants. Others know how to make the sand paintings that are an essential part of curing ceremonies. These paintings are created around the patient who sits on a hogan floor. The medicine man trickles powdered minerals of different colors and sacred corn pollen through his fingers onto sand. The medicine men are precise, patient, and have great memories. It takes four to six men several hours to make a painting about six feet across. The paintings are made after sunrise and destroyed before the sun goes down. There are singers who know one or more of the dozens of healing ceremonies. It is impossible for one medicine man to know and perform all the songs. Each ceremony lasts from two to nine days in which the singers chant and pray for hours.

Today, some Indian people go to see non-Indian doctors for broken bones and take non-Indian medicine for their illnesses. Medicine men and women recognize the value of non-Indian health care and have no difficulty referring a patient to a modern medical doctor for a problem. They believe, however, that even though someone has had surgery or medical treatment, that person is still not totally cured and may need a Native ceremony as well. They believe that although surgery or medicine may cure a part of the body that is disturbed, the patient must be rebalanced as a whole person in harmony with the universe.

Some medical doctors recognize that medicine men and women are important sources of medical techniques. Traditional healers know a great deal about the mind and spirit. They know how to deal with

George Hight, Museum of the American Indian, Heye Foundation
Grey Squirrel, Navajo medicine man, making a sandpainting

mental depression, anxiety, and people's fears. Indian medicine men and women have passed on valuable techniques to modern-day psychiatrists. Non-Indian medical organizations sometimes invite medicine men to speak at their medical conferences. Sacred healers have been invited to work alongside doctors treating patients at Indian Health Service hospitals and clinics.

Today, more and more Native Americans themselves are going to medical schools. In 1984, nearly 400 men and 127 women from Indian tribes and Alaska Native villages were practicing medicine in the United States. Some of them combine non-Indian science and health care with ancient Indian healing traditions.

9

Elders

Indian elders (people over sixty years old) consider aging a fact of life. They understand the forces of nature and accept that everything that lives also decays and dies.

Indian elders traditionally had a great deal of authority in their households and in their communities. They contributed experience, wisdom, knowledge, and skills to the family circle. They contributed knowledge and wisdom to their communities. They accumulated great experience in caring for children, understanding human nature, and governing people. They were honored and entitled to certain privileges that other tribal members did not have. They grew old in their homes surrounded by large families and did not go to old-age homes and retirement communities as so many non-Indian elderly people do today.

Elders had the right to give advice, lecture, and counsel younger people. They told and retold stories that taught the laws of their people. They told children legends that taught moral lessons. They told stories about the tribe's origins and where plants and animals came from. Elders were the "kindergarten, elementary, high school, and college" experience of young people.

The experience and wisdom of elders entitled them to be part of tribal governments. They served as the judges, lawyers, doctors, teachers, ministers, and politicians in their communities.

Today, many Indian people still regard Indian elders as valuable resources, storehouses of all that remains of the cultures, histories, and languages of Indian groups. Elders know how to conduct ceremonies properly, how to prepare healing remedies, how to speak the language. They know how to make objects of great beauty without patterns or blueprints.

In the past, elders have taken many traditional Indian ways to the grave because the information was stored in their memories. Today, all over the United States, many elders are recording legends, chants, languages, and other information in order to preserve their tribes' cultures for future generations.

Elders visit classrooms at Indian preschools, elementary and high schools, and community colleges, teaching classes and telling traditional stories during library hours. They attend youth-and-elder conferences and share their knowledge about traditional ceremonies, flute making, and tribal histories. In 1983, Inuit elders organized their own Elders Conference within the Inuit Circumpolar Conference. These Inuit elders dedicated themselves to the task of transmitting their knowledge to younger people.

Elders still play an important role in their communities. Many help raise their grandchildren. Others serve as foster grandparents to children without parents. Some elders work with younger tribal members who have health problems such as alcoholism.

The 1980 Census reported that there were about 109,000 Indian and Alaska Native elders sixty years old and older on reservations and in cities. The Census also revealed that sixty-one percent of the nation's Native American elders lived below the poverty line.

Many elders have serious problems. They have small incomes, in many cases only welfare payments, that do not permit them to live in good health and in dignity. Elders who live to be sixty-two receive small Social Security payments from the government as do all Amer-

Paul Conklin

A Navajo elder tells stories to children at a reservation school in Arizona

icans at this stage of life. Their homes do not have enough heat, or clean water, or decent plumbing. Often they do not have enough money for food or don't eat properly. Some live alone and cannot prepare their own meals, take medicine, or bathe and dress themselves. Some do not get the medical care they need. Many are without transportation and cannot get help from other elders who share the same concerns. Indian elders do not get legal assistance to help them write wills and fill out difficult government forms.

Many Indian elders have severe health problems. They suffer from tuberculosis, arthritis, diabetes, cancer, liver disease, and influenza. Many cannot see or hear and cannot afford dentures, hearing aids, eyeglasses, or counseling help.

There are not enough medical services and doctors, nurses, and dentists to treat Indian elders. There are not enough health care people who speak Indian languages. Often Indian elders cannot explain in English what is wrong with their bodies nor do they understand what doctors tell them. They do not understand why they are receiving injections, X-rays, and other tests.

A new kind of problem for elders in the twentieth century is the lack of concern younger tribal members sometimes have for them. As a result, some elders are depressed, isolated, and lonely.

In the 1970s, many Indian communities worried about the problems facing their elders. In 1976, close to 1,500 Indian and Alaska Native elders representing 171 tribes attended the first National Indian Conference on Aging. They spoke about their needs and made recommendations for ways to deal with their problems and improve the quality of their lives. The National Indian Council on Aging has had yearly conferences since 1976, and tribes are responding to the elders' recommendations.

The Gila River Tribe of Pima and Maricopa Indians in Arizona have a winter assistance program that provides blankets and firewood to elders who need them. Elders on this reservation formed their own housing committee. Twenty houses were constructed, grouped together so elders could be near one another.

The Papago Tribe of Arizona has tackled one of the toughest problems facing its elders, lack of transportation. The Papago Reservation has seventy-two villages scattered over three million acres, about the size of Connecticut. Some villages are as much as fifty miles from the next, connected by dirt roads. Most villages are far from medical clinics, and phones are often twenty miles away. Under the new program, tribal members transport elders to and from sites where meals are served and deliver meals to housebound elders. They shop for the elders and haul water, firewood, and hay for them. Young Papagos also take their elders to places where they can gather traditional desert foods and materials for making baskets.

64

In western Nevada, ten tribes have organized a homemaker service for elders. They deliver noon meals, shop for groceries, do laundry, and make beds. They bathe and dress elders and supervise medicine, take blood pressures, and teach about nutrition.

In 1982, the Laguna Pueblo of New Mexico dedicated the Laguna Rainbow Nursing and Elderly Care Center, a twenty-five bed nursing home. The Center sponsors a Home Health Program designed to keep elders out of the nursing home for as long as possible by sending licensed nurses into the elders' homes. Nursing care is a brand new experience for Indians. Traditionally, elders stayed in their own homes cared for by family members.

In cities, too, there are programs for elders. Urban centers provide meals as well as opportunities for elders to meet and socialize with one another. Some Indian centers help elders find ways to earn money.

After the National Indian Council on Aging was founded, other Indian elders created organizations that work to improve nutrition, transportation, legal services, and employment for elders. In 1978, Oklahoma Indians created the Oklahoma Indian Council on Aging to "bring about improved, comprehensive services to the Oklahoma Indian Elderly." In 1982, the California Indian Council on Aging was formed to improve the cultural, physical, social, and economic life of elders in that state, which has the largest population of aging Indians. In 1980 there were over 20,000 Indians sixty years and older in California, over eighty percent of which were unemployed and more than half of which had incomes below the poverty line.

Today, American Indian elders are experiencing a growing sense of urgency regarding their future in the midst of diminishing resources. Budget cuts and competition for funds threaten the existence of programs for aging Indians. The elimination of funds for transportation, health, and other programs threaten the very survival of Indian elders.

10

Children and Education

Indian children have grown up surrounded by large numbers of relatives. Parents, children, grandparents, aunts, uncles, and cousins live close together on reservations. Within these large families, children have lots of "substitute" relatives. Children call their mother's sisters mother, not aunt, as non-Indians do. Children call their father's brothers father, not uncle. Aunts and uncles treat nieces and nephews as their own children. Cousins treat each other as brothers and sisters.

In the past, many tribes had ceremonies for children at every stage of their lives, beginning with birth. These ceremonies were intended to help children live long lives. Though ceremonies differed from tribe to tribe, every group had naming ceremonies for infants and young children. Today, some tribes continue to have naming and renaming and puberty ceremonies for youngsters.

In the past, Indian families educated their children. Elders told and retold stories, legends, and myths that passed on to children survival skills and gave them practical information about avoiding poisonous snakes, poisonous plants, and dangerous cliffs. Through stories, children were taught to be unselfish, patient, generous, to respect elders and the environment, and how to worship. Indians valued this method of teaching children. Even today, many Indian elders educate their youth by telling and retelling stories, passing on their tribe's history and culture from one generation to the next. This is called an oral tradition.

Since the late eighteenth century, the U.S. government has tried to educate Indians. Government education meant getting Indians to think, live, and look like non-Indians, to stop being Indians. In 1775, the Continental Congress approved $500 to educate Indians at Dartmouth College. In 1819, Congress passed a law providing money to Christian missionaries who would "civilize" and "Christianize" Indians. In 1865, a Congressional committee recommended creating boarding (live-in) schools away from Indian communities where Indian children could be taught to think differently from their families.

By the late nineteenth century, the U.S. government had developed a system of federally operated schools designed to destroy the cultures of Indian children in places far away from the influence of parents, relatives, friends, and the tribal community. At the age of six or seven, children were required to go to government boarding schools.

By 1900, the government opened twenty-five industrial boarding schools. In these schools children were not allowed to wear tribal clothes or hairstyles or to worship according to their own tribal beliefs. They were not allowed to speak their languages. The schools tried to replace Indian cultures with the English language, with Christianity, and with vocations that were useless on a reservation.

In these schools, children were punished if caught speaking their tribal languages or trying to run away. They were made to stand on tip toes with arms outstretched for a long time or were locked in attics or basements without much food. Until 1930, boarding schools required strict military discipline. Children marched to meals and to classes, and they marched in their spare time to keep busy. Some children who were sent hundreds of miles away from home did not see their families for months and sometimes years. Children attending boarding schools on reservations went home during the summer.

In 1928, the famous Meriam Report was published. It attacked the boarding schools and suggested that day schools be built instead and that children be taught about their Indian cultures.

After the 1930s, the government stopped its organized attack on Indian cultures and languages, but a half century of boarding school experience had left many Indians bitter, hostile to schools, and out of place in their own tribes as well as in non-Indian society. Some Indians returned to their tribes and restored contacts with their own people and their traditional ways; others left their tribes and lived in non-Indian communities.

In the late 1960s, the Congress and the Bureau of Indian Affairs found that the problems pointed out in the 1928 report were still uncorrected. A group of senators began an investigation and in 1969 reported that Indian education was a "national tragedy."

> We are shocked at what we discovered. Others before us were shocked . . . others after us will likely be shocked, too . . . there is so much to do, wrongs to right, omissions to fill, untruths to correct.

The senators made sixty recommendations, including maximum participation and control by Indian parents and communities in their children's education. They recommended that Indian culture, history, and language be part of the curriculum, a recommendation the Meriam Report made in 1928.

During the 1960s, Indians who were educated in boarding schools began to realize that their culture, history, traditional beliefs, and languages were slipping away. Many young Indians were denying their heritage and losing respect for their sacred ceremonies. Indian parents began to realize their children needed a solid education in their tribe's culture, as well as in subjects required to live in the non-Indian world.

After 1965, Indian parents and educators spoke out against the past schooling of Indian children. They wanted to run their own schools.

With legal advice and assistance, they were able to contract with the Bureau of Indian Affairs to take over and operate schools.

In 1966, the Navajos established Rough Rock Demonstration School on the Navajo Reservation at Chinle, Arizona. It was the first Indian-directed, Indian-controlled school, and it belongs to local Indian people. Navajo educators developed a Navajo curriculum, teaching children about their way of life, language, and history. They also learn English and the history and culture of the United States.

In 1970, Montana Chippewas and Crees established the Rocky Boy Public Elementary School District. The school gave equal treatment to the culture and history of Chippewas and Crees and of the United States. Cree children study many of the same subjects that non-Indians do, but they also learn Cree music, legends, and language.

Paul Conklin

A school bus picks up Navajo children in northeastern Arizona, near Kayenta

That same year, a Navajo community of 1,200 people in western New Mexico started Ramah High School, the first Indian-controlled high school.

By 1975, Indians controlled fifteen more elementary and secondary schools all over the country. In the 1980s, Indian communities continued to organize schools.

Some Indian children, especially the Navajos, Crow, and Yupik Eskimos, speak tribal languages at home. They speak little or no English before they go to school and learn English as a second language. Teachers in Indian-controlled schools encourage children to speak Native languages, because it helps preserve the languages for the future.

Today, across the United States, Indian children attend different kinds of schools. Most Indian children go to public schools located on reservations, in Native communities, in rural areas, or in cities. The rest attend Indian-controlled schools like Rough Rock Demonstration School, mission or private schools, and Bureau of Indian Affairs–operated day and boarding schools, which now devote part of the day to teaching about Indian culture and history.

Before 1960, very few Indians completed high school, but in recent years Indians have graduated and gone on to college in increasing numbers. Indian educators have responded to this educational need by creating two-year community colleges on reservations. These colleges provide an alternative for Indian students who had to leave their communities to get an education after high school, and they offer courses about Native American languages, cultures, and histories.

In 1968, the Navajo Tribe created Navajo Community College (NCC). It was the first Indian-owned and Indian-directed community college located on a reservation. The Navajos who created NCC believe that Indian values, skills, and insights will contribute to the survival of the United States. The NCC campus design reflects Navajo philosophy. The Navajos oriented the campus to the east, and the

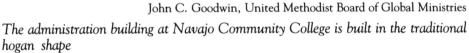

The administration building at Navajo Community College is built in the traditional hogan shape

main college road comes into the campus on the east side. The direction east represents thinking, reasoning, and planning to the Navajos. The campus designers also shaped the dormitories like hogans.

Since the 1970s, Indians have established nineteen Indian-controlled community colleges on reservations. In 1971, the Rosebud Sioux Tribe in South Dakota created Sinte Gleska College (SGC). Sinte Gleska is the Lakota (Sioux) name of Spotted Tail, an important Sioux in the nineteenth century. At SGC, students study the Lakota language and oral traditions. Graduates receive a hand-crafted buckskin diploma and a traditional eagle plume tied in his or her hair.

In 1970, President Richard Nixon told Congress in a special message on Indian affairs that Indian tribes should have the right to operate their own schools. In the early 1970s, Congress responded to

Indian educators who insisted on participating in their children's education, passing several bills that dramatically changed Indian education. For example, Congress passed the Indian Education Act of 1972. This bill stated that Indian parents and communities had to participate in creating education programs and curricular materials and in adult education programs. In 1975, President Ford signed a landmark law called the Indian Self-Determination and Education Assistance Act, requiring "maximum Indian participation" in education programs for Indian children. Now Indian parents serve on PTAs and school boards; they decide what their children will learn about Indian cultures.

11

Native Americans in Cities

In 1930, almost the entire Native American population lived on reservations. Only about ten percent of the population lived in cities. The 1980 Census reported, however, that over fifty percent of the Indian population lived outside reservations. These people were living in cities all over the United States, as well as in some rural areas. Most of the Indians, Inuits, and Aleuts live in large western and midwestern cities, but there are Indian populations in eastern cities like Baltimore, Boston, and New York.

According to the 1980 Census, the city with the largest American Indian population is Los Angeles, California, with over 82,000 Native people from dozens of tribes. Tulsa, Oklahoma, has the second largest Indian population with 32,000 Indians. Other cities with large Indian populations are Oklahoma City, Oklahoma (24,700), Phoenix, Arizona (22,800), Seattle-Tacoma, Washington (20,800), Albuquerque, New Mexico (20,700), New York, New York (20,500), Minneapolis-St. Paul, Minnesota (15,800), and Tucson, Arizona (14,900).

The cities listed above have larger populations than most reservations. Only the Navajo Reservation, with 132,000 Navajos in 1980, has a population greater than the Indian population of Los Angeles. In 1980, there were over 200 reservations with fewer than 1,000 Indians; 160 reservations had fewer than 500.

Large numbers of Indian people moved to cities because of U.S. government policies. In the 1940s and 1950s, the government tried to break up tribal life and get Indians to blend in with everyone else. The government promoted the idea that reservations had too many people. "Most of the reservations are greatly overpopulated, and could not support the present population at anything approaching a reasonably adequate American standard of living," reported a Congressional committee in 1954. The government was not willing to make reservations better places for Indians to live. It was willing, however, to place Indians at immense distances from their homelands so they could not return.

The Bureau of Indian Affairs sent officials to reservations to encourage Indians and Alaska Natives to leave their homelands and go to cities and get jobs there. The government officials called this program "relocation." The Bureau of Indian Affairs gave the "relocatees" one-way travel fare, housing, and money for living expenses while they looked for jobs. Between 1957 and 1966, around 50,000 Indians and Alaska Natives left reservations and relocated in cities. They ended up far from their homelands.

Indians who moved to cities had dozens of problems. They missed their families and friends, land, and community activities. Many Indians got low-paying jobs so they struggled to make enough money to pay the rent, buy food and clothes, and get decent health care. Many Indians got sick with pneumonia and viral infections. People could not understand Indian languages, and Indians were not familiar with English, so there was a language barrier. Indian children went to schools where teachers rarely understood their backgrounds and where other children rejected them. Some Indian students simply stopped going to school.

Thousands of Indians who relocated to cities stayed, and many more thousands have moved to cities in the 1970s and 1980s even though the government no longer encourages them to leave their reservations.

Mohawk men work on high beams at the Gimbel store in New York City

Many other Indians who relocated to cities have returned to reservations. Still others move back and forth between the city and reservation because of their jobs. For example, Mohawk high-steel construction workers in New York City finish work on Friday night and then drive seven hours to the Akwesasne (St. Regis) Reservation on the Canadian border. They spend the weekend on the reservation and return to work in the city on Monday morning.

Today, Indians mainly move to cities to get better education, housing, or jobs than they might get on reservations. Jobs pay more in cities than on reservations, but housing, food, clothes, and health care cost more, so the majority of Indians in cities do not improve their standard of living. Many miss their communities back home.

Indians have solved some of their problems by organizing Indian centers in dozens of cities. People at these centers help newcomers find jobs, health care, and housing. They explain city laws, how to take a bus, how to use pay telephones, how to get scholarship money for college. For example, the Detroit American Indian Center announced in February 1985 that "Emergency food and commodities are available every day. . . . If there are any other problems you may have, such as . . . not being able to make ends meet, trying to find the right agency to help you, utility shut offs, emergency housing or anything related, call me . . . and we'll help."

People from different tribes gather together at Indian centers and feast on traditional Indian foods. They learn job skills, study the English language, and dance at center powwows. After school and on

Virgil J. Vogel

The American Indian Center in Chicago, Illinois

weekends, centers run Indian culture and history classes for the whole family. These centers provide friendly company and opportunities to do Indian things in an Indian atmosphere.

Urban Indian centers differ from reservations because there are usually people from many different tribes that spend time at the centers. For example, the Boston Indian Council (Center) draws tribal members from all over the United States: Micmacs from Canada, Penobscots and Passamaquoddies from Maine, Sioux from South Dakota, Senecas and Mohawks from New York, Chippewas from Minnesota, Kiowas and Caddos from Oklahoma.

There are young Indians in cities who have never seen their reservations. They have never spoken their tribal language or gone to tribal ceremonies or listened to stories told by tribal elders. They are educated in city schools, away from their land and tribe. Some never develop an Indian identity.

But there are large numbers of Indians living in cities who continue being Indian. They feel that even though they have left their reservations, they have not given up being Indian. They hold on to their religion and language and take part in Indian activities in cities. They return to their reservations whenever possible to participate in tribal ceremonies and powwows and to visit with relatives and friends. They maintain close connections with their tribe, land, and customs.

12

Reservation Resources

Some natural resources—timber, soil, rangeland, water, oil, gas, and coal—play an important role in the economic life of tribes on hundreds of reservations. Rangeland and livestock operations, farming, mineral development, and forestry programs employ thousands of Indian people and also provide valuable incomes to tribes.

Some of the resources on reservations are renewable—that is, they can be restored. Renewable resources include water, timber, rangeland, and cropland. People can reforest, improve rangeland if it is in poor condition, and irrigate land so it can grow crops. Nature replaces water as rain and snow.

Some of the resources on reservations, like coal, oil, gas, and uranium, are nonrenewable. It is not possible to remake these resources once they are used up.

Water is a renewable resource that Indians consider a life-and-death matter, particularly in the dry western part of the nation. A governor of a New Mexico Pueblo explained that "Water is the lifeblood of our tribes, and if its life-giving flow is stopped, or it is polluted, all else will die. . . ." In 1976, Senator Edward Kennedy of Massachusetts said "[to] American Indians, land and water have always led the list of those materials deemed essential for both present livelihood and future survival. For Indians know that any threats to or dimunition of their

A Navajo flock drinks from a water hole on Black Mesa Reservation

land and water rights may constitute threats to their very existence. . . ."

Water has always been important to Indians. Over 2,000 years ago, for example, the Hohokams in the Great Salt River Valley diverted water by canals in order to grow plants. Present-day Pueblo Indians living in the Rio Grande Valley use water to grow crops in the desert environment. The Pimas and Papagos in Arizona today use sophisticated irrigation systems that permit them to grow crops. Tribes along the Colorado River use its water to irrigate crops. The Menominees of Wisconsin harvest wild rice from fields that line rivers. Indians of the Pacific Northwest live on salmon and other fish they catch from the Columbia River, and the Northern Paiutes of Nevada depend on fish they catch in the Truckee River and Pyramid Lake.

79

A large part of the Indian population in the West today depend on water for economic development and survival. Growing and selling crops is the only source of income for many Indians. Others make a living selling the fish they catch. Without enough water to nourish their lands, Indian farms will vanish. Without enough water in lakes and streams, Indian fisheries will vanish as well.

There is fierce competition for the small water supplies in the southwestern states of Arizona, New Mexico, and southern California. Indians and non-Indians alike need water. Non-Indian communities need water to produce food for the growing populations in western states and for city water systems, industry, coal mining, and grazing animals. Often these communities use water at a much faster rate than nature can replace it.

Around 1960, Rupert Costo, a Cahuilla Indian, warned Indians that "If we do not begin to act now, as Indian nations, to preserve our water rights, our nations will perish for lack of water. . . ." Recently, nearly every tribe in the western United States has had to fight with states to protect their water rights. They go to courts or they try to make settlements out of court. Court battles can last ten to twenty years and cost tribes and states millions in lawyers' fees.

Tribes count on two important past Supreme Court decisions in their battle for water. In 1908, the Supreme Court made a major water rights decision that has come to be called the Winters Doctrine Rights, which states that Indians are entitled to enough water on reservations to make their reservations liveable in the present and the future. In 1963, the Supreme Court ruled that Indian reservations on the lower Colorado River are entitled to enough water to irrigate all irrigable acres on their reservations.

For centuries, the O'odham in southern Arizona have been farming some of their lands with water from the Santa Cruz River. During the past few decades the river water has been depleted by operations of several copper mines, cattle ranches, and large non-Indian farms, together with use by the city of Tucson. Groundwater, too, was pumped in large quantities from beneath O'odham lands. O'odham fields began to dry up. In 1975 the tribe sued the mines, the city of Tucson, and all owners along the Santa Cruz River, demanding a halt to the theft of Papago water. Rather than fight for their water rights for decades in court, with an uncertain outcome, the tribe appealed to Congress to settle the dispute. Legislation passed by Congress in 1982 provides that water will be supplied by aqueduct from the Colorado River sufficient to farm twenty-five square miles of O'odham land.

Forests are another important renewable resource to Indians. There are over one hundred forested reservations in the country, totaling some fourteen million acres of forest land. The Yakima, Colville, and Fort Apache reservations contain about one-third of the total Indian forest lands. Timber is an important part of these and other tribes' economies. The tribal forest products enterprises on the Fort Apache, Navajo, Warm Springs, and Menominee reservations rank among the top 400 lumber producers in the United States and Canada.

Rangelands and croplands are also valuable renewable resources. The forty-four million acres of rangelands that Indian ranchers use for grazing cattle, horses, and other livestock make up almost eighty percent of the total Indian land base in the lower forty-eight. Indian reservations contain nearly three million acres of croplands, of which Indians farmed about one million acres in 1983. (Non-Indians farmed another one and a half million acres on Indian lands that they leased from tribes or Indian individuals.) There could be more Indian farming operations if there were improved irrigation systems. For example, tribes along the Colorado River only grow crops on ten percent of their land because of inadequate irrigation.

The supply of fish is a resource Indians are striving to preserve. Some tribes along the Atlantic and Pacific coasts have shell-fish hatchery operations. The Lummi Tribe of Washington State, for example, has a school of aquaculture at which Indians learn about managing fisheries and increasing the supply of fish.

Non-renewable resources on Indian reservations include coal, ura-

Animals grazing on Blackfeet Reservation in Montana

Harvesting lettuce on Salt River Reservation, Arizona

Bad River Chippewa Tribe in Wisconsin operates a factory that precuts logs for home use

nium, oil, and gas. There are coal deposits on over thirty reservations located in eleven states and oil and gas deposits on forty reservations in seventeen states. There are uranium deposits on twenty-five reservations, making up fifty percent of all known uranium reserves in the United States.

The demand for energy in the United States has increased every year as a result of a growing population and more industry. Some government leaders, hoping to lessen our dependence on energy from foreign countries, are urging the development of resources located on Indian reservations. Development can consume these nonrenewable resources, however, and damage the environment. Tribes are learning to balance development with the protection of their lands.

13

Economic Life

In 1970, President Richard Nixon told Congress:

> Economic deprivation is among the most serious of Indian problems. Unemployment among Indians is ten times the national average; the unemployment rate runs as high as 80 percent on some of the poorest reservations. Eighty percent of reservation Indians have an income which falls below the poverty line. . . .

In the 1980s, Indians continue to have severe economic problems. In 1980, between twelve and thirteen percent of the nation's population lived below the poverty line. In 1980, the Census Bureau estimated that there were 408,000 Indian people, or nearly twenty-seven percent of the total Indian population, living below the poverty line. This was more than double the nation's poverty rate.

A great many Indians are unemployed. In 1985, the government estimated that thirty-nine percent of Indians living on or near reservations were unemployed. On many reservations, the rate is higher. The Navajos, who live on the largest reservation, estimated that sixty percent of the work force was unemployed. The Sioux living on Pine Ridge Reservation, the second largest reservation, estimated that eighty percent of its work force was not employed.

Unemployment creates terrible problems. There are so few jobs and

Poverty on a California Indian reservation

so little money on some reservations that Indians cannot always buy the food and clothes they need. Some have returned to traditional ways of getting food, like hunting and fishing; others exchange necessities with neighbors, swapping food for blankets or wood.

There are very few Indian-owned businesses on reservations. This means that when Indians get their paychecks they must drive off the reservation to buy the things they need, pouring their dollars into the businesses and economies of non-Indian communities.

During most of the twentieth century, Indians on reservations got jobs in farming, stock raising, or forestry, but many can barely scratch out a living farming and ranching because of the General Allotment Act, which in 1887 broke up reservation lands into allotments, or small parcels of land. Tribes, individual Indians, or non-Indians may own these parcels. As a result, some reservations today have a checkerboard pattern of land ownership: one square owned by the tribe next to a square owned by a non-Indian next to a square owned by an individual Indian and so on. Tribes and Indians need thousands of acres to have successful farm and ranch operations, but in North and South Dakota, for example, allotments are only 160 to 640 acres. Many Indians have given up trying to farm or ranch on these small allotments. They sell off or lease their plots to non-Indians, or they do nothing with the land. On some reservations, non-Indians farm more land than Indians farm. In the northern plains and northwestern states, non-Indians graze livestock on rangelands leased from Indian tribes.

Tribes are trying to consolidate allotments into larger plots so they can operate profitable farms and ranches. The Crow Creek Tribe of South Dakota consolidated land and now cultivates 1,500 acres of alfalfa and winter wheat. Some tribes, however, lack money to buy land. The Lac du Flambeau Tribe of Wisconsin missed an opportunity to buy seventy-nine allotments because the tribe's income was too small.

During the 1960s and 1970s, the federal government urged industries to locate on reservations and provide jobs for Indians. In 1959, there were only three industrial plants on reservations, providing 391 jobs for Indians. In 1974, there were 250 plants on reservations that employed 6,173 Indians.

Many non-Indian businesses that locate on reservations hire non-Indians for jobs. Recently, some tribes passed regulations requiring all reservation employers to give preference to Indians for jobs. Before the Blackfeet Tribe of Montana passed an Indian-preference ordinance, construction projects on the reservation hired non-Indians; after passage of the ordinance, projects hired Blackfeet workers. This policy increased employment and gave Blackfeet people over one million dollars in salaries.

In the late 1960s and 1970s, tribes depended on the federal government to create programs on reservations, hire Indians, and pay their salaries. In the 1980s, however, Congress, at President Reagan's urging, made massive cutbacks in social programs and budgets of federal agencies. Among those eliminated were certain national economic assistance programs that aided Native American individuals, businesses, and tribes. Now there is less federal money and fewer jobs for Indians. The Oglala Sioux in South Dakota lost hundreds of federal job-training positions in the 1980s and now must find their own ways to develop their reservation economies.

Indians starting up their own businesses face many risks, just as non-Indians do. Many new businesses fail within their first year, even with well-located markets, experienced management and sales people, adequate financing, and good products. Sometimes the risks are greater for new reservation businesses. Many of them are built off the beaten path, far from highways or railroads, which decreases the number of customers. Even so, individual Indians and tribes have gotten loans and capital to start tribal farms, cattle ranches, arts and crafts shops, logging companies, sawmills, seafood-processing plants, wood-product factories, fisheries, and resorts. These businesses provide jobs for Indian men and women living on or near reservations.

Some tribes have acquired businesses. The Passamaquoddy Tribe of Maine has bought a cement factory, two radio stations, and the state's third largest blueberry farm. The Penobscots of Maine, along with the Passamaquoddies, have bought 300,000 acres of timberland. All these operations provide jobs for Maine Indians. The Mississippi Choctaw Indians created an industrial park in which three industries located. Nearly 700 Choctaws work there day and night, making electrical systems for trucks and autos and hand finishing greeting cards.

Since the late 1970s, there has been an explosion of Indian-owned businesses all over the nation. In 1985, a directory listed over 5,000 tribally and individually owned businesses in all fifty states. Indians grow wheat, corn, soybeans, lettuce, berries, and melons in sixteen

HAPPILY MAY I WALK

states. They operate commercial reindeer herds in Alaska, buffalo herds in four states, a hog farm in Idaho, a trout farm in North Carolina, and fish hatcheries in the Pacific Northwest and Great Lakes states. Indians operate forest nurseries, copper and coal mines, construction businesses, meat-packing and frozen-dessert plants, lumber mills, restaurants, and soap and glass-making plants.

The White Mountain Apaches of Arizona created the Apache Sunrise Ski Resort on their reservation. The resort employs 400 people, nearly eighty percent of them Apaches. The resort made four million dollars for the tribe in 1983. The tribe also operates the Fort Apache Timber Company, which has several hundred Apache employees. Despite these businesses, there is still around thirty-seven percent unemployment on the reservation. Similarly, though the Blackfeet Tribe of Montana runs a pen and pencil factory, hundreds of tribal members still leave the reservation to look for jobs, and in winter, seventy percent of the Blackfeet have no jobs.

Like other Americans, Indians and tribes have trouble borrowing money from banks, and because of the trust status of Indian land, it cannot be used as collateral. To remedy this situation, the American Indian National Bank, which makes loans to Indians and tribes, opened in Washington, D.C., in 1973. The Colville Tribe was able to purchase an expensive piece of drilling equipment and create a water-well drilling business with a loan from the bank.

However, tribes rarely get the money to buy the expensive equipment it takes to develop resources like coal, oil, and uranium. Tribes often do not have geologists, petroleum engineers, and other trained people working for them and must turn to outsiders to develop reservation resources. In 1983, tribes made 14,607 oil, gas, and mineral leases with companies.

Tribes are beginning to organize to protect their resources. In 1975, twenty-five tribes owning energy resources banded together to form the Council of Energy Resources Tribes (CERT). These tribes together

Utah International, Inc. mines coal on Navajo land outside Farmington, New Mexico

Some lumber mills pollute air and water

have more than fifty percent of all known uranium reserves in the United States, ten percent of all coal deposits, three percent of oil and gas production, and more than one third of strippable coal west of the Mississippi River. CERT tries to bring about energy laws that protect its interests and tries to get technical advice on developing energy resources. CERT encourages Indians to move into energy re-source–management professions. In 1980, the Jicarilla Apache Tribe of New Mexico, a CERT member, became the first tribe to acquire one hundred percent ownership of oil and gas wells on its lands.

Tribes want to preserve the beauty of their lands, but they also want to develop them, and it is difficult to do both well. Uranium mines contaminated a river that Navajos use for themselves and their live-stock. Coal mines have polluted the air. Oil spills have contaminated drinking wells and livestock ponds. On the Navajo Reservation, some former uranium miners have developed serious lung diseases. Tribes now must weigh energy development against the damage it does to their environment and health.

14

Treaty Rights

Treaties continue to play an important role in the American Indian world. A treaty is a legal agreement in writing between two or more nations acting as equals. The Constitution states that "all treaties made . . . under the authority of the United States, shall be the Supreme Law of the Land" and that "the judges in every state shall be bound" when a treaty is made, making it higher than a state law.

The British and Dutch made treaties with Indian nations long before the United States became a nation. After the Constitution became the law of the land in 1789, the United States made hundreds of treaties with many Indian nations. (It made over forty treaties with the Potawatomis alone and nearly forty with the Chippewas!) The Diplomatic Branch of the National Archives and Records Service has all the original treaties and will duplicate a treaty and send it to anyone who requests it and pays a fee. The Service will also answer questions about Indian treaties.

Important exchanges took place by way of treaties. The Indian nations gave up some of their political rights and large portions of their ancestral lands to the United States. In return, the U.S. government set up reservations for Indians. Some treaties promised Indians certain services, such as education, medical care, clothing, food, farm tools, and, in some cases, other lands. In the treaty between the United

States and the Navajo Nation, for example, signed on June 1, 1868, the United States gave the Navajos a carpenter and a blacksmith shop, a schoolhouse and chapel, clothes, and other goods in exchange for about seventy-five percent of Navajo ancestral lands.

National Archives

The first treaty between the U.S. government and an Indian nation: the September 17, 1778 treaty with the Delaware (Lenape) Indians

In 1871, Congress passed a law that ended treaty-making with Indian tribes, but that law also stated that treaties made with Indian nations before March 3, 1871 were still valid. Since 1871, Congress has regulated Indian affairs through laws, which do not require the signatures of Indians.

There is a great deal of controversy over treaties today. Some Indians would like tribes to start making treaties with the United States again; others feel the government should respect the old treaties. Some people in government believe that treaties with other nations have more importance than Indian treaties; some officials feel they have the right to change or even repeal an Indian treaty, just as Congress can end an international agreement. Then, too, there are federal officials and judges who believe that treaties still are the supreme law of the United States and that the government must not violate Indian legal rights written into treaties.

The U.S. government has broken nearly every treaty it has made with an Indian nation, usually to get Indian lands, and many Indian nations fight in and out of courts to try to get back lands illegally taken from them. For example, the Sioux tribes of South Dakota have fought for decades in the courts to get back the Black Hills, which were taken illegally by the U.S. government in 1877. In 1980, the government awarded the Sioux tribes $105 million—but not the Black Hills—to settle the claim. Many Sioux in South Dakota today want the land back, not the money. The Black Hills continue to be the spiritual center of the Sioux religious world. In July 1985, eight Sioux tribes supported a proposed bill to return land, including the Black Hills, illegally taken from them. There are also some Sioux who want to use the award money to buy land. It will take a long time to settle this dispute.

In most treaties written during the nineteenth century, the government guaranteed Indians the right to hunt, fish, trap game, gather wood, and harvest foods on and off reservation lands. (Off-reservation lands, which belonged to the Indians at one time, often contain foods that are important to religious ceremonies and the cultural heritage of tribes.) In the 1854 treaty between the United States and the Nisqually and several other tribes in present-day Washington State, for example, the tribes gave up land in exchange for their own reservation. Article 3 of the treaty promised the Indians "the right of taking fish at all usual and accustomed grounds and stations . . . in common with all citizens of the Territory . . . together with the privilege of hunting, gathering roots and berries, and pasturing their horses on open and unclaimed lands . . ."

During the twentieth century, non-Indians and industries have taken over "unclaimed" lands in many states. Non-Indians began competing with Indians for fish and game. Some non-Indians have tried to get treaties broken or abolished, and some states have refused to respect Indian treaties in regard to hunting, fishing, trapping, and gathering rights. State police have even been called in to stop Indians from fishing at their usual places, which is a treaty right.

Indians and states disagree over which government has jurisdiction over non-Indian fishing or hunting *on* reservations. Indians argue they have the right to regulate, restrict, and license hunting and fishing by anyone on their lands. States like Arizona, California, Minnesota, Oregon, and Washington have tried to regulate non-Indian fishing and hunting on reservations. Other states feel tribes have jurisdiction over non-Indians on their lands.

There is even more controversy over the treaty rights of Indians to hunt and fish *off* reservations. Many off-reservation fishing and hunting rights are granted by treaties made with Indians of the Pacific Northwest and the Great Lakes region during the mid-nineteenth century. The U.S. government gave Indians the right to fish at their "usual and accustomed places" and to hunt "on open and unclaimed lands." Thus, even as reservation lands were lost to non-Indians, Indian communities in the Northwest were still permitted to carry on their fishing and hunting activities. These communities continue to depend on fish for food, for their religious life, and for their economy.

Normally, a state has the authority to regulate fishing and hunting within its borders, but a treaty that permits Indians to fish off reservations cancels out state laws. States do not like this situation. They want their laws to govern Indians outside reservation boundaries, even if a treaty contradicts state law.

Indians and non-Indians fought for a century, often violently, over the issue of treaty fishing rights. There were serious disputes in Oregon and Washington State. Some of these battles ended in courtrooms with judges deciding what Indian fishing rights involved. In 1974, a U.S. District Court judge ruled that Indians in Washington State could catch all the fish they wanted on their own reservations and at traditional sites off the reservation. Now many non-Indian commercial and sport-fishing groups are angry because they must share fish with treaty Indians. In 1980, another U.S. District Court judge ruled that tribes have the right to fish in waters that are not polluted by sewage and chemical wastes, meaning that industries located near water must not pollute it.

In recent times, Indians have organized to protect their treaty fishing rights. The Yakima, Nez Perce, Warm Springs, and Umatilla Tribes in Oregon have created the Columbia River Inter-Tribal Fish Commission. Indian tribes in Washington State and the Great Lakes region have also organized to protect their fishing interests.

Today, Indians are concerned about non-Indians' violating their treaty rights to hunt and fish. They argue that the federal government should do more to protect these rights. Indians regard treaties as moral and legal statements that represent "the word of the nation" and protection from state interference.

15

Native American– U.S. Government Relations

One hundred and fifty years ago, the Supreme Court stated that the relationship of the United States to Indians was "perhaps unlike that of any other two people in existence." Today, the relationship continues to be unique.

The U.S. Constitution spells out the legal relationship between Indians and the U.S. government. It states: "Congress shall have the power . . . to regulate Commerce with foreign Nations, and among the several States, and with the Indian Tribes." The Constitution allows Congress to treat Indians in special ways because they are separate peoples with their own political institutions, not because of their race.

Over the years, Congress has passed thousands of laws affecting Indians. Some of these laws have been fair, but some have hurt Indians. For example, Congress has passed laws to make reservations smaller and has even abolished reservations altogether. In the nineteenth century, Congress abolished reservations in the East and relocated Indians to Oklahoma Territory and other lands. Sometimes, Congress passes laws that interfere with tribal governments. After 1885, Congress took away the tribes' rights to punish Indians who committed major crimes. At other times, Congress has simply abolished tribal governments: between 1954 and 1965 it ended the political institutions of over one hundred tribes. Congress has also passed laws that allow certain states to step into Indian tribal affairs, reducing tribal authority.

Congress has the power to treat groups of Indians differently by recognizing the existence of only certain tribes. Tribes that are recognized by the Congress are called "federally recognized." Federally recognized tribes are usually the ones that have made treaties, agreements, or other legal arrangements with the U.S. government.

As with state governments, the U.S. government carries on government-to-government relations with federally recognized tribes. It provides them with urgently needed programs and health, education, housing, and legal services. In April of 1984, there were almost 300 federally recognized tribes in the United States. In addition, there were about 200 Alaska Native villages that had the same rank.

Tribes that never have made treaties or agreements with the government are not recognized and do not receive government services. Though they are unrecognized, many of these groups have some form of government, a tribal language, customs, religion, and a long history. The names of some unrecognized Indian communities are the Chickahominy Indian Tribe in Virginia, the Lumbees of North Carolina (the largest unrecognized group in the country), the Mashpee Wampanoags of Massachusetts, the Pennacooks of New Hampshire, and the Wintus in California. There are over 140 Indian groups, with over 100,000 individuals, who are not recognized by the U.S. government.

Unrecognized Indian groups may petition the government for recognition. They must satisfy requirements for recognition established by the Department of the Interior. If a group manages to win recognition, it is entitled to receive the same programs and services available to other federally recognized Indian tribes. In January 1973, eighty Apaches in Arizona won their struggle to gain federal recognition as a tribe, and they became eligible for federal programs such as fire protection and electricity. In June of 1973, 250 Coushattas of Louisiana received federal recognition as a tribe, enabling them to receive important health, education, and economic development programs. In the mid-1970s, ninety-seven Jamul Indians of southern California were granted recognition, as were 1,750 members of the Confederated Tribes of Siletz Indians of Oregon.

The U.S. government has refused to extend some services to federally recognized Indians who live in cities. These Indians would receive these services if they lived on their reservations. Many government people argue that if Indians leave their reservation, they should use services available to the general public. Indians argue that they should have the special government services even if they do not live on reservations, that they continue to be Indian wherever they live. But the U.S. government has elected to serve on-reservation Indians more than Indians in cities.

It is impossible for Congress to tend to Indian affairs on a day-to-day basis, so federal agencies were created to do the work. These federal agencies are responsible for carrying out the many programs and protecting Indian rights.

Congress has given the Secretary of the Interior a great deal of power over Indian trust lands, lands that the government holds "in trust" for Indian tribes. Without the trust protection, reservations could be sold off by individuals and disappear, so the government is supposed to protect this land for Indians. The government's responsibilities stem from treaties, solemn agreements, and promises made to tribes in return for land. Tribes and individual Indians with trust lands must get permission from the Secretary of the Interior to sell trust lands. If Indians or tribes want to lease trust lands, the Secretary of the Interior, as trustee, approves or denies each lease. The Secretary of the Interior, with the agreement of the tribe, approves or denies the building of highways, pipelines, or power lines across reservation lands.

The Bureau of Indian Affairs is the most important government agency in Indian affairs. Congress created it in 1824 as part of the War Department. In 1849, Congress switched the agency to the newly created Department of the Interior, where it has been located ever since.

The Bureau of Indian Affairs has its central office building, officers, and staff in Washington, D.C., and has twelve area offices located throughout the country. The only area office to serve a single tribe is the Navajo area office, which is located at Window Rock, Arizona. The Eastern area office, headquartered in Washington, D.C., directs Bureau of Indian Affairs operations in New York, Connecticut, Rhode Island, Maine, North Carolina, Louisiana, Mississippi, and Florida. There are eighty-four Bureau of Indian Affairs agencies located on reservations that work directly with tribes on a daily basis. The agency superintendent is the essential link in the government-to-government relationship. The Bureau of Indian Affairs has the primary responsibility for carrying out the trust responsibility and Indian programs in education, community development, economic and resource development, law enforcement, upkeep and building of new roads, housing, and others.

Many Indians and Alaska Natives work for the Bureau of Indian Affairs. At the end of 1984, there were about 16,000 Bureau of Indian Affairs employees, almost eighty percent of whom were Native people.

The largest part of the Bureau of Indian Affairs budget is for education programs. The Bureau of Indian Affairs funds over 175 schools for over 40,000 Indian students. The Bureau of Indian Affairs supports day schools, on- and off-reservation boarding schools, and schools run by tribes; it provides money to public schools for Indian students; and it gives scholarship grants to thousands of Indian college students. The Bureau of Indian Affairs also assists nineteen tribally-controlled community colleges and runs three post-secondary schools: Haskell Indian Junior College in Lawrence, Kansas; the Institute of American Indian Arts in Santa Fe, New Mexico; and Southwestern Polytechnic Institute at Albuquerque, New Mexico.

Many Indian people are unhappy with the Bureau of Indian Affairs. They feel that the agency does not do enough to protect their land

Joseph C. Farber

Cherokee Indian Hospital is administered by the Indian Health Service, part of the U.S. Public Health Service

and natural resources. They resent the fact that the Bureau of Indian Affairs sometimes does not consult with Indians concerning how to improve their conditions. But Indians do not want the Bureau of Indian Affairs destroyed.

The Indian Health Service (I.H.S.) is another important federal agency serving Indians. The Bureau of Indian Affairs took care of Indian health until 1955 when the I.H.S. was set up in the U.S. Public Health Service. The I.H.S. was created because tuberculosis, diabetes, influenza, pneumonia, and infant death rates are higher for Indians than for other groups in the population. Native people still have many health problems. As in many other communities, alcohol and drug abuse are serious health threats.

The I.H.S. provides health services to more than 960,000 American Indians and Alaska Natives living on or near federal reservations and in Oklahoma and Alaska. It runs forty-seven hospitals, eighty health centers, and more than 500 smaller health stations. Thirty-seven health projects in cities refer Indians to the proper health-care providers.

Sometimes, it is difficult for Indians in remote areas to get to I.H.S. offices. Roads are bad or do not exist at all, people do not have cars, or they are too old or too ill to drive. For these reasons, most reservations have ambulance services. Native Americans in cities, which may have no Indian clinics, often do not get medical care at all. They may not know what services the city provides, or they may have been mistreated by non-Indian health-care people and refuse to go for help.

In 1976, Congress passed the Indian Health Care Improvement Act to help Indians become doctors, nurses, dentists, and other kinds of health-care providers. The Act was designed to bring Indian health care up to the level of the rest of the nation, but Congress has not provided enough funds for I.H.S. programs. The I.H.S. has done much to improve the health of Indians, but it still does not have enough health-care workers to give proper medical care. Some I.H.S. hospitals need to be modernized, and new hospitals and clinics need to be built. Some I.H.S. clinics are overcrowded. For example, on the Washington State Yakima Reservation one year, 38,000 patients went to a clinic that was built to receive only 18,000.

There are many more federal agencies with Indian programs for which tribes are now eligible. There are programs for Indians in the Department of the Interior, including the U.S. Fish and Wildlife Service, U.S. Geological Survey, the Bureau of Mines, the Bureau of Reclamation, the Indian Arts and Crafts Board, and the National Park Service. Besides the Department of the Interior, other government departments run Indian programs: Housing and Urban Development, Health and Human Services, Education, Labor, Agriculture, Justice, Commerce, Treasury, Defense, Energy, and Transportation. In 1980, the Bureau of Indian Affairs and other federal agencies spent three billion dollars on Indian programs, one-third of which was spent by agencies in the Department of the Interior.

Besides federal agencies, federal courts (district courts, twelve courts of appeal, and the Supreme Court) make legal decisions that affect Indian reservation land, water and minerals, religious life, hunting and fishing rights, tribal taxing power, and other important areas. Since 1959, the Supreme Court has made seventy-five Indian legal decisions, more decisions than the Court has made in areas like pollution or international law. All of these legal decisions affect the daily lives of Indian people.

16

Native American– State Government Relations

Almost every Indian reservation is located within the boundaries of a state. Only a few reservations are in more than one state, like the Navajo reservation, which is located in three states, or the Standing Rock Sioux Reservation, located in two states. Each state has the right to regulate all people and activities within its borders—with one exception: states usually cannot control the activities of Indians on reservations located within their borders.

States cannot regulate the activities of tribal businesses on reservations or tax their income. States cannot require Indians to pay state taxes on money they earn working on reservations or on things they buy within reservation borders. States cannot require Indians to buy state hunting and fishing licenses on reservations, they cannot regulate marriages or divorces of Indians living on reservations, and they cannot tell Indians how to use their reservation lands.

If an Indian leaves a reservation, however, he or she must obey state laws like everyone else. If a tribal business moves off a reservation, it has to pay taxes like any other business.

Today, many non-Indians live on Indian reservations, and states can tax and regulate these residents. States tax non-Indian owned land that is within the boundaries of Indian reservations, and they tax non-Indians leasing Indian lands.

John C. Goodwin, United Methodist Board of Global Ministries

The dividing line between the lands of the state of New Mexico and an Indian reservation

For a long time, states and tribes have resented each other. States resent Indians on reservations, because they do not have to pay various taxes. States claim this causes them financial hardship. Indians, for their part, have resented state governments that have tried to tax and regulate them. Although many states and tribes do get along, there are still squabbles over which government—tribe or state—has jurisdiction (the right to administer a region) over Indian reservations.

States have two basic powers within their borders—criminal and civil jurisdiction. Criminal jurisdiction involves making laws about illegal actions within state boundaries, while civil jurisdiction means making laws to control the everyday life of people (civil matters). States would like to make laws that regulate criminal and civil matters on Indian reservations, but they cannot unless Congress gives permis-

104

sion. Congress has, at times, allowed states to enact criminal laws for Indian reservations.

In 1953, Congress passed a law permitting five states—California, Minnesota, Nebraska, Oregon, and Wisconsin (Alaska was added in 1958)—criminal jurisdiction over Indian reservations. The law permitted several other states to have criminal jurisdiction over Indian reservations if they chose. As a result, Indian justice systems in certain states could no longer punish their own criminals, who were dealt with by state courts and laws.

The federal government has also taken some jurisdiction away from tribes. Congress had passed several crime acts, which have given the government power to punish Indians on reservations who commit any one of fourteen major crimes such as robbery, murder, or arson. Once again, the authority of Indian justice systems was removed.

State governments have also tried to extend their civil laws into Indian country, but the Supreme Court usually resists any such attempt. The Supreme Court has said that states cannot interfere in day-to-day affairs of tribes unless Congress gives permission. On a few occasions, Congress has allowed New York State and Oklahoma to extend their civil laws over Indians within their borders. Basically, tribes have jurisdiction over their members in civil matters, and states cannot interfere in tribal marriages, divorces, adoptions and child custody arrangements, taxing, or land-use ordinances.

States cannot extend their civil laws over non-Indians doing business on Indian reservations. A non-Indian who owns a trading post on an Indian reservation obeys the tribe's civil laws, not the state's laws. Tribes can tax non-Indian companies taking oil and gas from reservation lands and can tell non-Indians how to use the land. Non-Indians can be prevented from selling alcohol on reservations, and non-Indian businesses on reservations must observe tribal health and safety rules. Even a non-Indian just passing through a reservation must obey the tribe's civil laws until he or she leaves. As the Supreme Court stated in

1980, Indian tribes have a "broad measure of civil jurisdiction over activities of non-Indians on Indian reservation lands."

Sometimes, Congress allows states to pass civil laws that apply to non-Indians on reservations. For example, states can insist that Indian storeowners on reservations collect a state sales tax from non-Indian customers. States can also insist that Indian shopkeepers make records of their sales to non-Indians and turn these records over to the states.

States provide many services to Indians, as they do to all people living within their borders. States provide schools, mental hospitals, nursing homes, prisons, and other services for Indian people. Tribes simply do not have the money to operate all these institutions. Even though Indians living on reservations do not pay state taxes, states cannot refuse to provide services to them.

In most states with Indian tribes within their borders, there is a state agency that works with Indian people. The Alabama Indian Affairs Commission, the Connecticut Indian Affairs Council, and the Florida Governor's Council on Indian Affairs are examples of these agencies. People working for these state agencies can answer various questions about Indians within their borders.

During the past fifteen years, tribes in Maine, Connecticut, New York, Rhode Island, Massachusetts, and South Carolina have claimed that in the eighteenth and nineteenth centuries their lands were taken illegally by states. In the past, states had the right to negotiate for Indian lands within their borders, but the federal government was supposed to supervise and approve all land transfers from tribes to states. Sometimes, the federal government did not supervise the transfers, which makes them illegal. Several Indian tribes have proved their land was taken illegally. The federal government and some states have paid tribes millions of dollars to settle the land claims.

The Penobscots and Passamaquoddies of Maine settled the largest land claims case in the eastern part of the nation. It took the tribes ten years to find a lawyer willing to represent them. Finally, in the early 1970s, the tribes found a lawyer who eventually proved the tribes' claim that their lands were taken illegally in 1794, 1796, and 1818. In 1980, the claim was settled through legislation, and the tribes won eighty-one and a half million dollars as payment for lands taken without Congress' approval. The money helped the tribes buy 300,000 acres in Maine.

In 1979, the Narrangansett Indians of Rhode Island were the first tribe to settle a major land claim on the Eastern Seaboard. The tribe won about three million dollars, which permitted them to buy 900 acres of private land. Rhode Island donated another 900 acres in the settlement.

In 1983, the Mashantucket Pequots (also known as Western Pequots) settled their land claims case. The tribe, located in Ladyard, Connecticut, proved that in 1855 800 acres of their land were sold illegally. The tribe received $900,000 from the federal government. The tribe used two-thirds of the amount to purchase land. Connecticut agreed to contribute twenty acres to the tribe and to provide money for road building and repair services to the reservation.

One Indian land claims case went all the way to the Supreme Court. In 1985, the Oneida Tribe of New York proved that 872 acres were taken illegally in 1795. Arlinda Locklear, Lumbee attorney, represented the tribe before the Supreme Court. She is the first Indian woman to argue a case before the Supreme Court.

Not every tribe settles its land claims case in its favor. The Mashpee Tribe of Wampanoags in Massachusetts tried to recover land in the town of Mashpee that it claimed was taken illegally. The tribe lost its case in 1978.

17

Termination
and Self-Determination

During the last forty years, the U.S. Congress has had two major—but contradictory—Indian policies. The first policy, which guided government officials in the 1950s and 1960s, has come to be called "termination." The second policy, "self-determination," has been guiding government officials since the mid-1970s.

In the late 1940s, some federal officials wanted to assimilate, or absorb, Indians into non-Indian society. Some officials felt that well-off tribes did not need a special relationship with the U.S. government. At that time, both Indians and Congress were unhappy with Bureau of Indian Affairs services. Officials discussed reducing government expenses by shifting federal programs to states. Other government people blamed reservation poverty on the reservation system. They felt the special government-Indian relationship prevented Indians from getting ahead and that the Bureau of Indian Affairs was another useless and wasteful federal agency.

Indians believed government officials wanted to terminate tribal governments so that non-Indians could get Indian lands. They believed that the federal government wanted to save money by getting rid of its treaty obligations and responsibilities to protect Indian lands and peoples.

By the early 1950s, many government people wanted to end federal aid to Indian tribes. On August 1, 1953, the Eighty-Third Congress declared that termination was the official Indian policy of the United States and that it intended to end the special relationship between Indians and the government as well as end the special tax-exempt status of Indian lands.

Congress's resolution began with these words:

> Whereas it is the policy of Congress, as soon as possible, to make the Indians within the territorial limits of the United States subject to the same laws and entitled to the same privileges and responsibilities as are applicable to other citizens of the United States . . .

Congress singled out certain tribes for immediate termination:

> . . . at the earliest possible time all of the Indian tribes and the individual members . . . located within the states of California, Florida, New York, and Texas and all the following named Indian tribes and individual members . . . should be freed from Federal supervision and control . . .

The Flatheads of Montana, the Klamaths of Oregon, the Menominees of Wisconsin, the Potawatomis of Kansas, and other tribes were listed. The resolution was written to sound attractive to people, but the destructive parts of the policy were not detailed.

To Indians, termination meant "to be wiped out." The first tribe to be terminated was the Menominee Tribe of Wisconsin. Congress passed the Menominee Termination Act in June of 1954. The law abolished the tribe's government and made tribal members and land subject to state laws. The law stated that no new Menominees could be enrolled into the tribe. Therefore when the last enrolled member of the tribe died, the Menominee people would no longer exist—at least from the government's point of view. The government directed the Menominees to use their own money to hire experts to show them how to survive after termination. Once all tribal property was divided among Menominee members, the tribe was officially terminated, and individual members of the tribe were not entitled to any of the services performed by the United States for Indians. A group of Menominees felt they were wiped out, because certain government officials wanted "to see us rapidly assimilated into the mainstream of American society—as tax-paying, hard-working, 'emancipated' citizens."

Between 1954 and 1966, "the termination era," Congress terminated over one hundred tribes, most of them in Oregon and California. Termination affected more than 11,500 Indians and one and a half million acres of Indian land. Most of the terminated tribes were small. Thirty-seven terminated California reservations had an average of thirty members. Several large tribes, too, were terminated. The Menominees had more than 3,000 members and owned 233,000 acres of land. The Klamaths of Oregon had 2,133 members and 863,000 acres.

Termination was a short-lived policy, but it was a disaster for Indian tribes. The tribes were no longer eligible for federal Indian services. They had to dismantle their own governments and distribute all tribal property to tribal members. After this, the tribe no longer existed as a political body. All tribal members became subject to state laws. At the same time tribes were being terminated, the Bureau of Indian Affairs launched a massive program to relocate reservation Indians to urban centers. This was part of the federal plan to dissolve tribes. Most termination activities were carried on without the consent of tribes. A 1977 government report stated that "oppressive tactics were utilized by the B.I.A. to secure tribal consent for termination."

After termination, the Menominees were required to pay state taxes immediately on lands that had been protected by federal trust status. The Menominees had to pay counties for road maintenance and police protection. They could not pay the enormous bills, and poverty was the result, as well as higher rates of infant deaths and tuberculosis, poor housing, and mediocre schools.

110

By 1972, the Bureau of Indian Affairs concluded that a "return of the Menominee Tribe to the trust relationship with the Federal Government is the only solution to this hopeless situation." The Menominees established an organization to work with the state of Wisconsin to get termination reversed. In 1973, Congress repealed termination of the Menominees, restoring the tribe to federal trust status and services.

The termination policy produced poverty on reservations that were "ended" and insecurity on reservations that were not officially terminated and still had a relationship with the federal government. As one Indian spokesperson explained in 1967, it was impossible for Indians to plan anything when the Bureau of Indian Affairs constantly threatened to terminate them. In 1973, Vine Deloria, Jr., Sioux spokesperson, told a U.S. House Committee, "I think that the fear of termination has become almost psychopathic among Indian people. . . . You ask [tribes] why they do not want certain developments, and they will say, well, we do not want to build something else up that is going to be taken away in several years by some type of termination legislation."

During the last fifteen years, the U.S. government has not repealed the Congressional resolution on termination, but it has tried to reverse the policy. In 1970, President Richard Nixon announced that the official federal Indian policy would be "self-determination." First he explained the reasons for rejecting termination.

The policy of forced termination is wrong . . . for a number of reasons. First . . . termination implies that the federal government has taken on a trusteeship responsibility for Indian communities as an act of generosity toward a disadvantaged people and that it can therefore discontinue this responsibility . . . whenever it sees fit. But the unique status of Indian tribes does not rest on any premise such as this. The special relationship between Indians and the federal government is the result . . . of solemn obligations which have been entered into by the United States

111

Government. Down through the years, through written treaties and through . . . agreements, our government has made specific commitments to the Indian people . . . the special relationship . . . continues to carry moral and legal force . . . the second reason for rejecting forced termination is that the practical results have been clearly harmful . . . [tribes'] economic and social condition has often been worse after termination than it was before. The third argument . . . concerns the effect it has had upon the overwhelming majority of tribes . . . The very threat . . . has created a great deal of apprehension among Indian groups. . . .

During the 1960s, there was increasing awareness of the problems of Native Americans and other minorities. Activist Indians began occupying sites such as Alcatraz, the Bureau of Indian Affairs building in Washington, D.C., the town of Wounded Knee, and others. Native American organizations were created to promote Indian interests. In 1961, Indians from over sixty tribes gathered in Chicago and declared that Indians wanted the right to participate in developing their own programs. The federal government responded. During President Lyndon Johnson's administration, Indians were included in the "War on Poverty" programs. Reservations received millions of dollars under the Economic Opportunity Act, which allowed tribes to design their own programs to meet community needs. In 1966, President Johnson appointed Robert Bennett, an Oneida from Wisconsin, Commissioner of Indian Affairs. He was the first Indian in almost a century to hold that office. During the 1970s, many Indians were hired at high-level agency positions.

In 1968, President Johnson delivered a special message to Congress about the problems of American Indians. He proposed self-determination, a new goal that would end the debate over termination. He wanted Indians to have "An opportunity to remain in their homelands, if they chose, without surrendering their dignity; an opportunity to move to towns and cities of America, if they chose . . ."

In 1970 President Nixon urged Congress to allow Indian communities to control federal Indian programs operating on their reservations. Nixon said that "Indians can become independent of Federal control without being cut off from Federal concern and Federal support."

During 1970 to 1973, Congress restored land and trust status to certain groups. Sacred Blue Lake was restored to the Taos Pueblo of New Mexico in 1970. The Yavapai Apaches of Arizona received federal recognition and a small eighty-five acre reservation in 1971. In 1972, the Stockbridge-Munsees of Wisconsin regained 13,000 acres of land, and the Yakimas of Washington State regained more than 20,000 acres of sacred timberland. In 1973, the Menominees of Wisconsin were restored to federal status, and the Tiguas of Texas were federally recognized. In 1975, President Ford restored land to the Havasupais of Arizona.

In 1975, Congress passed the Indian Self-Determination and Education Assistance Act. It contained a short statement rejecting termination, and it emphasized a commitment to "maintenance of the federal government's unique and continuing relationship with Indian people." This act gave Indian tribes the right to operate federal programs formerly provided by the Bureau of Indian Affairs. Today tribes operate over one-half of all Bureau of Indian Affairs programs themselves.

Despite the 1975 law, a congressman from Washington State introduced a bill in 1977 that called for termination of every Indian tribe. It did not pass Congress. In 1983, the American Farm Bureau Federation adopted a similar resolution. The termination threat still exists.

18

Arts

American Indians and Alaska Natives have always expressed themselves artistically. Their clothing, pottery, blankets, and dwellings were all shaped and decorated with great skill and patience. But Native Americans did not have art classes, museums and galleries, or famous artists. Tribes did not single out anyone as gifted because she or he created a perfect object. Creating beautiful designs on household objects was such a natural part of life that traditional Indian languages did not even have a word for art or artist. Among the Northwest Coast Indian groups, however, people who might be considered artists worked for wealthy chiefs. Their wood carvings, totem poles, and utensils were designed to make the chiefs famous for having such magnificent possessions.

Some tribes restricted the creation of sacred artwork to people who had proper training and talent or religious background. These people spent their lives painting sacred art in ceremonial *kivas* (round, underground chambers), on pipes, medicine bags, and special clothes worn in ceremonies. They carved sacred masks. Symbols, or secret codes, were often used on religious objects, but many of these symbols are not understood today. The Indians who knew the meanings of sacred designs have died and left very few written records. The decorations on everyday objects do not have secret meanings.

Long ago, Indians practiced various ritual acts before they created an object. For example, Zunis carved sacred masks from wood that came from trees struck by lightning. Before carving, they prepared the trees in special ways, "addressing" the tree and "feeding" it tobacco. Zunis believed the rituals were as important as the skills they used to carve the masks.

Today, many Native Americans continue to practice rituals before they create. Before firing a pot, a potter offers prayers that the fire won't damage the object. A basketmaker prays while collecting grasses. Although many potters, sculptors, beadworkers, weavers, basketmakers, painters, and jewelers continue ancient ways, they combine their traditions with modern techniques and materials to create new art forms.

People throughout the world know the ceramic art of Pueblo Indians of New Mexico. For thousands of years, they have created storage jars for food and water, canteens, and pitchers, all decorated with stylized animals, birds, plants, and geometric patterns. Some of today's potters experiment by embedding turquoise beads in the clay, and some dry their clay pots in electric ovens. But other potters work with materials in the same way their ancestors did. They gather clay and sand, yucca for paint brushes, and other plants for making paints. They shape vessels by blending ropelike coils of clay with their hands. Besides the Pueblo people, tribes in other parts of the United States make pottery as well. The Mississippi Choctaws, whose pottery traditions stretch back almost one thousand years, still practice the craft.

Long ago, Native Americans sculpted various materials into everyday or ceremonial objects. The Haidas and Tlingits and Tsimshians carved cedar wood in the Pacific Northwest, the Hopis carved stones and cottonwood they found in present-day Arizona, and the Inuits in Alaska carved ivory and bone. Today, Native American sculptors use wood and stone as their ancestors did, but they also use aluminum, bronze, soapstone, and marble.

Paul Conklin

A Navajo woman making a basket

In traditional times, Native Americans used natural materials to make beads. Inuits in the Arctic used mammal teeth, Indians in the Northeast used clam shells to make wampum beads, and Indians in the Southwest made turquoise beads. Today, Native Americans continue to make beads of natural materials, but they also use beads of glass or other manufactured materials to make jewelry or decorate everyday or ceremonial objects.

Pueblo Indians developed weaving techniques in the Southwest over a thousand years ago. They influenced Navajo Indians, and now Navajo women are world famous for their woven rugs and blankets. Different styles of Navajo weaving have developed in different parts of the Navajo Reservation. "Two Gray Hills," with geometric patterns and natural wool colors, is a well-known Navajo design.

Native American basketmaking is one of the oldest occupations in the world. People made baskets in all sizes and shapes. They were used to catch and wash fish; to carry babies, equipment, and seeds; and to store food and clothes. Baskets were made of grasses, yucca leaves, cattails, willow, cane, roots, bark, cedar, spruce, and oak, and some were woven so tightly that they held water. People gave baskets at weddings and funerals. There were endless designs and ornaments like feathers, bells, seashells, and beads.

Today, only a few Native Americans continue to make baskets in the ancient ways with traditional shapes and designs. People in the Apache, Pima, Papago, Hopi, and other groups still make fine baskets that require time, effort, and patience. In 1980, there were about a dozen Haida basketmakers left in southeastern Alaska. They keep Haida basketmaking alive by passing on all they know to younger students and to scholars.

Painting is not a new art form to Native Americans. Tribes in every part of the nation painted religious and everyday objects, but they were not for display. People decorated objects for sacred reasons or to please themselves. Today, however, Native American painting is very different from that of long ago.

Indians paint canvases that are hung in museums and in art galleries and published in books. They use modern art techniques, composition, and color to express traditional subjects. Paintings show the lifeways, rituals, dances, legends, and other traditions of the tribes. Most Indian painters today depict their tribes' cultures because they know them best, but some Indian artists avoid traditional subject matter altogether so they are identified simply as artists, not Indian artists.

Ancient Indian peoples made and wore necklaces, bracelets, and ear pendants. Today, Indian jewelers use their ancestors' methods and western metal-working techniques to create their own jewelry.

Indians of the Southwest create world-famous jewelry. Navajo jewelers, after studying Mexicans working with silver in the mid-nineteenth century, began to make bold turquoise-and-silver pieces that people wear all over the world. Santo Domingo Pueblo jewelers produce *heishe*, handcut turquoise and shell that are ground into beads. Zunis set stones into silver channels and polish them flat. Hopis use an overlay technique in which two pieces of silver, the lower one blackened, are melted together. The top layer has cut-out designs.

Today, many traditional Native art forms are dying off. In some

Pena Bonita

A painting by Pena Bonita of Roslyn Wallace, the first Native American woman ironworker

Paul Conklin

A Navajo silversmith at work

tribes, younger people are not interested in creating objects that require enormous amounts of time, energy, skill, and patience. There
are fewer and fewer elders alive who possess the knowledge required to
turn out objects of great skill and beauty.

Contemporary Native American artists have borrowed from other
people's traditions. Indian women in the northern Plains observed
quilting done by missionaries and American settlers in the late nineteenth century, and they transformed quilting into an art form of their
own. They created the Plains Indian morning star quilts that have
bold geometric patterns borrowed from hide paintings, porcupine quill-
ing, and beading. The star design on the quilts represents the morning
star, the beginning of a new day, or a new life. Indians use these quilts
in ceremonies; they give them at birth, wear them in death, and give
them to honor people. They exchange them at "give-aways," when

119

families gather from different reservations to sing, dance, and feast on traditional Indian foods and to give gifts.

Inuits have their own rich tradition of art forms. The ancestors of contemporary Inuits made beautiful hunting tools, household objects, and clothing. In the seventeenth century, Inuits traded these goods with whalers, explorers, and traders. Today's Inuit art forms have grown out of this history of making and trading useful objects. Inuit animal lore, stories, and legends also influence their creations. Today, Inuits carve ivory tusks into human and animal figures. They scratch pictures into ivory tusks and carve ivory into useful objects like scrapers, game boards, and knives.

Native Americans now study in art schools all over the country. Many of them go to the Institute of American Indian Arts in Santa Fe, New Mexico. Founded in 1962, this is one of the world's best colleges of fine arts. The school's literary magazine has been ranked among the best in the nation, and many of the Institute's graduates have received international fame and prizes at major art exhibitions.

Native Americans with one-quarter or more Indian blood do not have to pay tuition, room, and food expenses at the Institute. Around 200 students attend the school, studying painting, printmaking, photography, film and video, sculpture, graphics, jewelry, ceramics, and weaving. Courses also include dance, creative writing, Native American studies, and museum training. The Institute's museum training graduates get jobs in tribal and city museums across the nation. The Institute has its own museum, which exhibits art and cultural objects from the present and past.

In Alaska, the Institute of Alaska Native Arts was created in 1976. The Institute has developed programs in visual, performing, and literary arts. It encourages both traditional and contemporary Alaska Native art forms. For example, the Institute sponsored a five-day skin sewing workshop. Thirty-two skin sewers shared their skills, knowledge, and patterns. The Institute has also sponsored spruce root and birch bark basketry workshops.

Kenneth B. Metoxen, Courtesy Institute of American Indian Arts Museum

Nail and Wood Porcupine by Sammy Sandoval, Jr., Navajo student at the Institute of American Indian Arts

Today, dozens of art books show pictures of traditional and contemporary Native American art forms. Many tribal communities own and operate their own arts and crafts centers, where they sell hand-crafted objects. Indian and non-Indian museums all over the nation exhibit ancient Native objects and contemporary art forms.

The Indian Arts and Crafts Board, an agency located in the Department of the Interior in Washington, D.C., promotes Native American arts. It runs three museums, publishes books, and tries to educate the public about fake Indian art. The Board encourages people to buy Native American arts by publishing a directory of Native American–owned and operated arts and crafts businesses.

19

Performing Artists

Today, many Indian and Alaska Native people work in the performing arts. This field includes dancing, music, film-making, and theater.

Traditionally, Indians prayed through ceremonial dancing. They danced for peace, in joy and sorrow, to give thanks for harvests. It is natural that contemporary Indians express themselves by dancing.

Five American Indian women, all from Oklahoma, have become internationally famous ballerinas. Maria Tallchief, Osage, danced her first solo when she was fifteen years old in the Hollywood Bowl and was the first American to dance with the Paris Opera Ballet at the Bolshoi Theater in Moscow, Russia. She danced before President John F. Kennedy and kings and queens of Europe. Maria Tallchief's sister, Marjorie, is also a prominent ballerina. Roselle Hightower (Choctaw), Yvonne Chouteau (Cherokee), and Moscelyne Larkin (Shawnee-Peoria) have also gained fame through ballet.

Some Indians have combined ancestral Indian and contemporary dance into new creative expressions. For example, Moscelyne Larkin has fused American Indian dancing and Russian ballet forms. Rosalie Jones, a Blackfeet from Montana, studied traditional Indian and contemporary European dance concepts and created three dance productions combining the forms.

Many Indians have made contributions to classical, jazz, folk, rock, country-and-western, and gospel music. Louis W. Ballard, a Quapaw-Cherokee, composes music using Indian themes. He has written several Indian ballets. One of them, "Four Moon," was presented in Tulsa, Oklahoma, on October 28, 1967, Oklahoma's sixtieth anniversary of statehood. His symphony, "Why the Duck Has a Short Tail," is based on a Navajo folk tale. Ballard's cantata, "Portrait of Will Rogers," was nominated for the Pulitzer Prize in music in 1972.

Carlos Nakai, Navajo-Ute flutist, blends traditional Sioux, Blood, and Zuni melodies with contemporary elements. He has captured the haunting sounds of the flute in his first album, "Changes."

Bonnie Jo Hunt, Sioux, was a world-famous opera star. At one time, she sang with the San Francisco Opera. Now she leads the Artists of Indian America, a group of dancers, opera singers, and actors that tour the nation, conducting workshops and giving performances.

Buffy Sainte-Marie, Cree, is an internationally-known folk-singer, composer, poet, and frequent visitor on TV's "Sesame Street." Her songs often protest the injustices done to Indians by the U.S. government. For example, in "Now That the Buffalo's Gone," she tells how the Senecas of New York lost a battle with the U.S. government over the Kinzua Dam, which flooded thousands of acres of Seneca reservation land when it was built.

Floyd Westerman, a Sioux folk-singer and musician from South Dakota, also protests against injustices suffered by Indians. During the 1970s, he gave many concerts on college campuses and at Indian pow-wows. His first album, called "Custer Died for Your Sins," was released in 1970. Paul Ortega, an Apache musician from New Mexico, has combined traditional Apache singing with guitar rhythms instead of the traditional drum and he, too, sings many protest songs.

There are many Indian rock groups. XIT has released several albums, including "Plight of the Redman" and "Silent Warrior." Steve and Lee Tiger, Miccosukee brothers who grew up in Florida, created a rock band called Tiger-Tiger, which plays both contemporary rock and traditional Miccosukee music. Tiger-Tiger recorded an album in 1980 called "Eye of the Tiger." Redbones, Winterhawk, Sand Creek, and Many Hogans are other American Indian rock groups.

Native American country-and-western groups and gospel groups are numerous. Among the former are Navajo Clan, Navajo Sundowners, The Thunders, and Apache Spirit. Gospel groups include the Arbor Shade Gospel Singers (Navajos), Smith Family Gospel Singers (Cherokees), American Indian Hymn Singers (Creek), and Harvey Family (Navajo).

Many albums by these recording artists are available from companies that specialize in American Indian and Alaska Native music. Canyon Records of Phoenix, Arizona; Folkway Records of New York, New York; and Indian House of Taos, New Mexico, carry large collections of Native American music.

A few Indians have become successful actors and entertainers. William Penn Adair Rogers, better known as Will Rogers, a Cherokee from Oklahoma, appeared on stage, screen, and radio. He wrote six books and a column that appeared in 350 daily newspapers, and he lectured widely. When he died in 1935, he was the country's highest paid film and radio personality. Will Rogers continues to entertain people. His radio programs have been reproduced on tape cassettes and records. He made more than seventy motion pictures that are shown on television and at film festivals. Rogers once joked: "My ancestors may not have come over on the Mayflower but they met 'em at the boat." A statue of Will Rogers in Claremont, Oklahoma, bears his best-known statement: "I never met a man I didn't like." Oklahoma has made Will Rogers Day, November 4, a legal holiday.

Jay Silverheels, a Mohawk from Canada, was famous for his role as Tonto, sidekick to the Lone Ranger in the television series, and also performed in movie westerns. He founded the Indian Actors Workshop in Los Angeles in 1966 and campaigned to make the movie and television industry aware of qualified Indian actors. In 1979, Silverheels became the first American Indian to have his star set in Hollywood's "Walk of Fame" along Hollywood Boulevard. He died in 1980.

In 1970, Chief Dan George, the seventy-one-year-old Tse-lal-watt Indian from Canada, was named Best Supporting Actor by the National Society of Film Critics and received the New York Critics Award for his role in the film "Little Big Man." He played the role of Old Lodge Skins, an elder who observed the destruction of Indian people by brutal non-Indians.

Will Sampson, Oklahoma Creek, is an actor and a self-taught painter. Mr. Sampson's performance credits include an Academy Award nomination for his role as Chief Bromden in "One Flew Over the Cuckoo's Nest" and numerous television appearances. He narrated "Images of Indians," a Public Broadcasting Service series dealing with stereotyping of Indians by the film industry. He has long been a role model for hundreds of young aspiring American Indian actors and actresses.

Charles Hill, Oneida from Wisconsin, acted in Indian theater groups such as the Native American Theater Ensemble and Red Earth Performing Arts that perform across the nation. In the 1970s, he became a stand-up comic. He uses American Indian experiences in his routines whether he is on television or in nightclubs.

There are over half a dozen American Indian theater companies producing plays, touring, and sponsoring workshops and classes. A few examples are the American Indian Theater Company located in Tulsa, Oklahoma; the Indian Time Theater Company located at the Native American Center for the Living Arts at Niagara Falls, New York; the Native American Theater Ensemble in residence at the Los Angeles Actors' Theater; and the Thunderbird Theater Company, located at Haskell Indian Junior College in Lawrence, Kansas.

In the 1970s and 1980s, Native Americans got involved in making their own films. A handful of independent film and video-makers document Native American cultures and contemporary life. They produce the films for Indian and non-Indian audiences.

Phil Lucas, Choctaw, feels that film-making is a natural extension of Indian culture. "Everything we did was 'show and tell,' using visual image, oral skills, and drama," he says. He feels making films is the best way for Native Americans to express themselves. He produced the first television series about Indians that was broadcast nationally. Through interviews and filmclips, his "Images of Indians" explained just how "Hollywood" Indians were created by the non-Indian film industry.

Chris Spotted Eagle, Choctaw, produces films about the Native American experience. He produced "Our Sacred Land," a half-hour documentary about a sacred mountain in South Dakota called *Mato Paha* by the Sioux and Bear Butte by non-Indians. The film appeared on public broadcasting television stations in 1985. Spotted Eagle explains that although film and video are not traditional Indian art forms like pottery, weaving, and painting, what he brings to the screen reflects Indian attitudes.

The Native American Public Broadcasting Corporation, established in 1977, encourages the creation, production, promotion, and distribution of quality programs by, for, and about Native Americans. The Corporation raises money to get films produced about Indians. It trains Native Americans in film and television and sponsors a national Indian media conference.

Some tribal groups produce their own audio-visual materials. For example, the Choctaws of Mississippi produced several videotapes about the tribe today. These tribal audio-visual departments also create materials for classrooms.

In 1984, a group of Indian actors created the American Indian Registry for the Performing Arts. The Registry tries to connect the hundreds of highly trained and talented Indian performers with producers, directors, and casting agencies who have work to offer. The Registry

126

publishes a newsletter that circulates information about film and television production plans, casting information, Indian theater seasons, new albums, concert tours, and other material to help people find work. The Registry wants to change the fact that a large share of the roles in films about Indians are filled by non-Indians and that moviemakers do not use Indian people to help them make the setting and story line accurate. The Registry hopes to eliminate the excuses of producers, studios, and networks who claim they cannot locate Native Americans to work in film. In its first two weeks of existence, the Registry was asked to locate Indians for more than twenty positions on one film.

20

Sports and Powwows

Throughout their history, Native American children and adults have entertained themselves by playing games that require skill and strength. Sports were often practiced for fun, but they also helped youngsters develop skills that helped them survive while they were hunting or protecting their communities from enemies.

Today, Indian youngsters participate in sports to have fun, to learn skills, and to bring honor to their communities. A coach at Little Wound High School in Kyle, South Dakota, explains that Indian teenagers "run and play ball for the good that it will bring to our families, community, and our school. It will bring pride to our people. . . . It helps our young want to grow up and do great things; makes them aspire to greatness. . . ."

Running is a popular athletic activity for Native American young people. There are cross country running teams at Indian high schools and community colleges. Indians like to play lacrosse, kickball (a relative of soccer), and stickball, all of which they played long ago. The Choctaws of Mississippi have a yearly stickball championship at which several communities on the reservation compete for the title of world champions. Native Americans swim and box and ride in rodeos. They play baseball, basketball, football, table tennis, golf, and hockey.

Native American communities honored their athletes long ago, and

Paul Conklin

Choctaw men play their national sport, stickball, during the Choctaw Fair in central Mississippi, where their reservation is located

Boys on the Sisseton-Wahpeton Sioux Reservation in South Dakota watch a baseball game in comfort

Pena Bonita

they continue to honor them today. In 1972, a group of Indians founded the American Indian Athletic Hall of Fame located on the campus of Haskell Indian Junior College in Lawrence, Kansas. The Hall of Fame represents America's outstanding Indian heroes in amateur and professional sports. The first induction was in 1972. So far, fifty men and one woman have been inducted into the Hall of Heroes, which is part of the Hall of Fame. A plaque represents each athlete, with a picture and accomplishments etched on each plate. Here are the names, tribal affiliations, and sport each "hero" has excelled in to earn the honor of being included in the Hall of Heroes.

Amos Aitson	Kiowa	football, boxing
Alexander Arcasa	Colville	football, lacrosse
Charles Bender	Chippewa	baseball
Sampson George Bird	Blackfeet	football, track and field
David W. Bray	Seneca	lacrosse
Ellison Brown	Narragansett	marathon runner
Elmer Busch	Pomo	football
Wilson Charles	Oneida	track and field
Chester L. Ellis	Seneca	boxing
Albert A. Exendine	Delaware	football
Harold Foster, Jr.	Navajo	track and cross country
Virgil R. Franklin	Arapaho-Kiowa	boxing
Robert L. Gawboy	Chippewa	swimming
Joseph N. Guyon	Chippewa	football
Albert Hawley	Gros Ventre-Assiniboine	football
Robert T. Holmes	Ottawa	football, track and field
Gordon A. House	Navajo-Oneida	boxing
Stacey S. Howell	Ottawa	football, track and field

Frank Hudson	Laguna Pueblo	football
Jack Jacobs	Creek	football
Clyde L. James	Modoc	basketball
Jimmie Johnson	Stockbridge-Munsee	football
Walter Johnson	Paiute	football
Nelson B. Levering	Omaha-Bannock	boxing
George Levi	Arapaho	football, basketball, track
John Levi	Arapaho	football
Wallace Littlefinger	Sioux	track and field
John Meyers	Cahuilla	baseball
William Mervin "Billy" Mills	Sioux	track and field
Rollie T. Munsell, Jr.	Chickasaw	boxing
Phillip Osif	Pima	track, cross country
Bemus Pierce	Seneca	football
Frank Mt. Pleasant	Tuscarora	football
Jessie Renich	Choctaw	basketball
Allie P. Reynolds	Creek	baseball
Theodore Roebuck	Choctaw	football
Ed Rogers	Chippewa	football
Angelita Rosal	Sioux	table tennis
Joseph H. Sahmaunt	Kiowa	basketball
Reuben Sanders	Tututni-Rogue River	football
Elyah Smith	Oneida	football, baseball, track
Louis Tewanima	Hopi	track and field
Joe Tindle Thornton	Cherokee	archery
Jim Thorpe	Sac and Fox	track and field, football
Austin B. Tincup	Cherokee	baseball

Egbert Bryan Ward	Yakima	football, baseball, basketball
Gus Welch	Chippewa	football
Louis Weller	Caddo	football
Martin F. Wheelock	Oneida	football
Jimmie Wolf, Jr.	Kiowa	football
Thomas Cornelius Yarr	Snohomish	football

The six men who developed the Hall of Fame have also received honorary memberships.

Native American athletes have astonished the world in the Olympic Games in the twentieth century. In 1912 at the Stockholm, Sweden, games, two Indians, Jim Thorpe and Louis Tewanima, were stars. Thorpe, Sac and Fox, won the gold medal in the pentathlon and the decathlon. Thorpe has been called the "Greatest Athlete of the Twentieth Century," and there is even a town in Pennsylvania named after him. In 1984, the U.S. Postal Service honored Thorpe with a commemorative stamp, and he became the first football player to be so honored. Tewanima, Hopi, won the silver medal in the 10,000 meters run. In the 1932 Olympics, Wilson Charles, Oneida, won fourth place in the decathlon. In 1936, Ellison Brown, Narragansett, who won the Boston Marathon that year and later in 1939, was a member of the U.S. Olympic Marathon Team. In 1948, Jessie Renich, Choctaw, was captain of the gold medal U.S. Olympic basketball team. And in 1964, William "Billy" Mills, Sioux, stunned the world when he won the gold medal in the 10,000 meters race at the Tokyo, Japan, Olympic games. He is the only American to win the event.

Patti Lyons Catalano, Micmac, is another famous long-distance runner. Her second-place finish in the women's division of the 1981 Boston Marathon set an American record.

Since 1961, the Inuits and Indians in Alaska have had the World Eskimo-Indian Olympics, several days of athletic games of strength,

132

Powwow dancing is popular across the United States

endurance, concentration, and quickness. Some of the events are the Toe Pull, Kneel Jump, Knuckle Hop, Arm and Ear Pull, One Foot High Kick, Blanket Toss, Eskimo and Indian Stick Pull, and the Greased Pole Walk. In addition to the games, there are dance and art competitions and contests for fish cutting, seal skinning, and muktuk (an Inuit food treat) eating, plus other traditional athletic games. Some of these games were used by elders long ago to teach young people the cultural values of their society and certain skills, such as how to survive the subzero Arctic environment and long, dangerous hunts for food. For example, some games trained hunters how to cross sea ice. Hunters had to be able to jump from ice floe to ice floe in case the sea ice on which they were traveling broke away from shorefast ice.

When Indians get together today, in cities or on reservations, they connect and communicate through dancing, especially at powwows, a popular social event among Native Americans. Powwows, as they are called today, started in the 1950s and 1960s in the Plains region when Sioux, Crow, Blackfeet, and other Plains tribes gathered together for fun and dancing. This intertribal social event has spread to most tribes, providing opportunities for Indians from different tribes to meet. People exchange traditional songs and dances and discuss the meanings behind them. They feast on Indian food and participate in dancing, singing, and drumming competitions, art shows, games, and sports.

There are many different kinds of social dances at these get-togethers. One of the most popular is the men's Fancy Dance, in which the men use fast and elaborate dance steps and wear brightly colored clothes. There are women's shawl dances, men's traditional dances, and tiny tot dances.

There are powwows for just about every occasion: to raise money for Indian organizations; to celebrate holidays; to honor elders, children, and Vietnam Veterans. Some draw thousands of people. They are held all over the country, indoors and outdoors, at Indian centers in cities, Indian clubs at colleges, and reservation communities. Newspapers published by Indians on reservations and in cities carry schedules of powwow events, and everyone is welcome to attend.

21

Native American Organizations

Native Americans have decided one of the best ways to promote their interests is to band together and create organizations that try to influence policymakers at all levels of government. In the twentieth century, American Indian and Alaska Natives have formed dozens of organizations of all sizes. They may be composed of only Indians or of both Indians and non-Indians. Some are national organizations; some are regional or state groups. Here are examples of a few national Indian organizations.

In 1968, the American Indian Movement (AIM) was founded. The organization began as an urban Indian program in Minneapolis, Minnesota, to help Indians overcome problems of adjusting to city living. AIM patrols, young Indian men and women wearing red jackets, patrolled Minneapolis streets to prevent police from mistreating Indians. Today, AIM is a national activist organization with chapters in many states. AIM members protest violations of tribal sovereignty and treaty rights. For instance, AIM occupied the Bureau of Indian Affairs building in Washington, D.C., in 1972, and it occupied the town of Wounded Knee, South Dakota (on the Pine Ridge Sioux Reservation), in 1973. AIM members work at restoring pride in being Indian, which they feel is a matter of cultural survival. They are willing to use violence and conflict to get recognition of their goals. Some tribal leaders approve of AIM and its methods, but many do not.

135

In 1974, the International Treaty Council was founded to protect treaty rights of all tribes. The Council sends delegations to international meetings concerned with the rights of Native people. The Council also takes its fight for Indian rights and sovereignty to the United Nations. For example, Thomas Banyacya, Hopi, delivered a message before a U.N. Conference on World Habitat. He appealed to the world to support the Hopis in their struggle to resist destruction of their sacred lands and life by energy companies.

In 1944, the National Congress of American Indians (NCAI) was founded. Today, over 200 tribes from all over the nation belong to this group, which tries to influence government agencies and Congress to protect Indian rights. In the 1950s, the NCAI fought against termination policies. It now fights for the protection of land, natural resources, and treaty rights and for cultural survival.

Bureau of Indian Affairs

A session at a convention of the National Congress of American Indians

In 1961, the National Indian Youth Council (NIYC) was founded. Thousands of Indians from reservations and rural areas have joined the NIYC. The group's purpose is to make young Indian people active members of their tribal communities, particularly by becoming involved in politics at the tribal, state, and national levels.

In 1970, the National Tribal Chairman's Association was founded. Only elected officials of recognized tribes belong to this group, which insists that the Bureau of Indian Affairs, the Indian Health Service, and other federal agencies protect the rights of recognized tribes.

In 1976, the National Urban Indian Council was founded. It represents over 200 urban Indian groups and works with city, county, state, and federal agencies to make them responsive to the needs of Native Americans living off reservations. This group provides Indians with information about city services and technical assistance.

In 1970, the Native American Rights Fund (NARF) was founded. It is an Indian law firm that works directly with Native American tribes, groups, or individuals in cases of major importance to all Indian people. Since 1970, NARF has brought 1,000 cases before the country's court systems on behalf of Indians. NARF protects tribal resources like land, water, minerals, and game, and it defends the rights of prisoners in jail.

There are many other national Indian organizations, including the Americans for Indian Opportunity, the Association on American Indian Affairs, and the Indian Rights Association. Some regional groups are the Affiliated Tribes of Northwest Indians, the All-Indian Pueblo Council, the Arizona Inter-Tribal Council, the Columbia River Inter-Tribal Fish Commission, the Great Lakes Inter-Tribal Council, and the United South and Eastern Tribes.

Alaska Natives have also organized several groups. The Alaska Federation of Natives (AFN) was organized in 1967. Members of this organization include the Alaska Native regional corporations and other Native organizations in Alaska. The AFN works with the Bureau of Indian Affairs, Congress, the state of Alaska, and private companies that are interested in Alaska's natural resources. It played a key role in the Alaska Native Claims Settlement Act of 1971 (see Chapter 3).

In 1977, Alaska Inuits along with Inuits from Greenland and Canada organized the Inuit Circumpolar Conference (ICC). The ICC established a special membership for Soviet Inuits until they are able to join officially. The group defends Inuit culture and has developed its own policies to influence the governments of the United States, Alaska, Canada, and Greenland regarding such issues as energy and economic development, environmental protection, education, and culture. For example, the ICC calls for bans on nuclear testing, missile placement, uranium mining, nuclear waste dumps, and "nuclear devices" in the Arctic.

In 1983, thirty-six Alaska Native tribal governments organized the United Tribes of Alaska (UTA). The member tribes intend to protect the sovereignty of tribal governments in Alaska.

Some Indian organizations are special-interest groups—that is, they are concerned with one subject area, such as health care, education, energy, or housing. Here are a few examples of these organizations:

• The American Indian Higher Education Consortium. All the two-year Indian community colleges join this organization, which represents the colleges' interests and tries to get funding from Congress to improve higher education for Native students.

• The Council of Energy Resources Tribes (CERT). Over thirty tribes with various energy resources belong to this organization. The tribes banded together to ensure that Indian people get a fair price for their energy resources. CERT assists tribes in protecting their resources from the effects of energy development, and it encourages young people to enter professions involving development and protection of natural resources.

• The National Indian Council on Aging. It works to improve services to Indians and Alaska Native elders. The Council has run several conferences on aging. It testifies before Congress about elders' needs, and it provides elders with information about available services.

• The National Indian Health Board. It assists Native Americans in obtaining health care. Members of the Board are elected Indian officials with a strong understanding of the field of health care. The Board works with Congress and the Executive branch to improve the delivery of health services.

• The Native American Science Education Association. Its members are Indian and non-Indian educators who feel there is a critical need for tribal members trained in engineering and scientific resource management. The organization encourages Native Americans to explore careers in science and math.

There are dozens of other groups for Indians and Alaska Natives. There are groups for nurses, doctors, social workers, cattlemen, judges, educators, women, performing artists, museums, public broadcasters, athletes, businesses, and journalists, and many, many more.

22

Writers and Journalists

Creating poetry and telling stories have always been important parts of Native American life. In the Inuit language, the word meaning "to make poetry" is also the same word for "to breathe," and countless Native Americans have considered poetry as important as breathing. Long ago, however, Indians did not write their poems on papers—they chanted or sang them out loud. Sometimes, drums or rattles accompanied the chanting poet. Indian people created poems for every occasion—for times of peace, mourning, planting crops, hunting, or honoring a special person.

Native Americans traditionally have been avid storytellers. It was a universal practice among them to teach through stories that related information about the cultures and histories of tribes. Stories taught skills, about good and bad behavior, about the creation of the world. These stories were not written down, but were recited out loud, with plenty of body movements, facial expressions, and different tones of voice. Native Americans admired people who could deliver a good story and valued the imagination necessary to communicate through spoken words.

The poems that Native American people chanted and the stories that Native American people told are called oral literature, because it was spoken and not written. Today, American Indian and Alaska

Native poets and novelists draw on this rich heritage of oral literature. They have converted the literature, however, into a written form and now use English to create their poems and novels.

Some Indian writers have been honored by Indians and non-Indians alike for their storytelling abilities. In 1969, N. Scott Momaday, Kiowa, won the Pulitzer Prize for Literature for his novel, *House Made of Dawn.* The literary world has praised novels by James Welch, Blackfeet, and Leslie Marmon Silko, Laguna Pueblo. A book of poetry by Wendy Rose, Miwok-Hopi, was nominated for a Pulitzer Prize in 1980. Louise Erdrich, Chippewa, won the National Book Critics Circle Fiction Award in 1984 for her novel, *Love Medicine.*

Publishing of Native American poetry and fiction is a twentieth-century development, but Indian newspapers, newsletters, and journals have been available since the early nineteenth century. Newspapers enable Indians within one tribe or across the nation to communicate with each other. Newspaper writers try to build unity among tribes.

The first Indian paper, the *Cherokee Phoenix,* was published in a New Echota, Georgia, print shop in 1828. It was printed in both the Cherokee language and English. The *Phoenix* ceased publishing in 1834, but since then over one thousand Indian newspapers, magazines, quarterlies, annuals, and newsletters have been founded. Many of them publish for only a short while and then go out of business. In the early 1960s, there were fewer than twenty papers; in 1984, there were about 400 newspapers, newsletters, magazines and other kinds of publications aimed at Native American readers.

Some newspapers are published by tribes for a select audience—their own tribal members. Examples of tribal papers are the *Lac Courte Oreilles Journal,* published monthly by the Wisconsin Chippewas, the *Fort Apache Scout,* published monthly by the White Mountain Apaches of Arizona, and the *Navajo Times Today,* published daily Monday through Friday by the Navajo Tribe. The *Navajo Times Today* is circulated over an area the size of New England. Mark N. Trahant,

141

A selection of tribal newspapers

Shoshone-Bannock editor of the paper, was honored by the National Press Foundation in 1985 with a special citation for "an inspiring display of individual journalistic initiative" in remaking the former tribal weekly into a daily keyed to Indian concerns.

Besides tribal papers, there are some publications that cover several tribes. *The Lakota Times,* a weekly, carries the news of fourteen reservations in North and South Dakota and Nebraska. *The Tundra Times,* a weekly, focuses on Alaska Native news.

It is difficult to get a complete picture of national Indian news without reading dozens of tribal papers. However, one newspaper, called *Akwesasne Notes,* carries selected news about Indians all over the United States, Canada, and Central and South America, and about Native peoples in other nations. Its articles protest mistreatment of Native people everywhere.

Many Indian organizations, community colleges, and Native American studies programs at universities publish journals. For example, the

National Congress of American Indians publishes the *NCAI News*, the Association on American Indian Affairs publishes *Indian Affairs*, the Indian Rights Association publishes *Indian Truth*, the Native American Rights Fund publishes the *NARF Legal Review*, and the Native American Studies Program at the University of California at Berkeley publishes the *American Indian Quarterly*.

Most Indian centers in cities print newsletters. Many of these publications do not survive beyond an issue or two. Only a few urban centers have full-fledged newspapers like the one published by the Los Angeles Indian center, *Talking Leaf*. Published for over forty years, *Talking Leaf* contains news articles about local, state, and national Indian affairs, a calendar of events, poetry, help-wanted ads, and lists of agencies that provide help, Indian churches, health clinics, powwow dates, and schools with Indian studies.

In 1984, forty Indian journalists formed the Native American Press Association (NAPA). This national organization was created to help distribute news to different Indian newspapers efficiently. NAPA hopes to encourage Indians to enter the field of journalism and plans to honor Indian journalists, editors, photographers, advertising people, and newspaper publishers with awards every year. At NAPA's first convention in 1985, it made Overall Excellence Awards to *How-Ni-Kan*, published by the Potawatomis of Oklahoma, *Siletz News*, published by the Siletz of Oregon, the *Seminole Tribune*, published by the Seminoles of Florida, and *Spilyay Tymoo*, published by the Warm Springs Tribes in Oregon.

Several libraries in the United States collect newspapers, magazines, and other publications published by Indians on reservations or in cities. The Princeton University library in New Jersey, the Museum of the American Indian library in New York, the Newberry Library in Illinois, the Smithsonian Institution in Washington, D.C., and the State Historical Society of Wisconsin have the most extensive collections.

Further Reading

GENERAL

Allen, Terry, editor. *The Whispering Wind: Poetry by Young American Indians.* Garden City, N.Y.: Doubleday, 1972.

Ashabranner, Brent. *To Live in Two Worlds: American Indian Youth Today.* New York: Dodd, Mead, 1984. Photographs by Paul Conklin.

Deloria, Vine, Jr. *God is Red.* New York: Dell, 1973. A contemporary philosophical discussion of American Indian religion by a Sioux author.

Gridley, Marian E. *Contemporary American Indian Leaders.* New York: Dodd, Mead, 1972.

Katz, Jane B., editor. *This Song Remembers: Self-Portraits of Native Americans in the Arts.* Boston: Houghton Mifflin, 1980.

Kavasch, Barrie. *Native Harvests: Recipes and Botanicals of the American Indian.* New York: Random House, 1979.

Leitch, Barbara. *A Concise Dictionary of Indian Tribes of North America.* Algonac, Mich.: Reference Publications, 1979.

Marquis, Arnold. *A Guide to America's Indians: Ceremonies, Reservations, and Museums.* Norman: University of Oklahoma, 1978.

Naylor, Maria. *Authentic Indian Designs.* New York: Dover, 1975.

U.S. Department of the Interior, Indian Arts and Crafts Board. *Native American Owned and Operated Arts and Crafts Businesses: Source Directory.* Photographs of arts and crafts sold by Native Americans all over the United States.

Wood, Margaret. *Native Fashion: Modern Adaptations of Traditional Designs.* New York: Van Nostrand Reinhold, 1981. Instructions for making contemporary clothes, by a Navajo-Seminole author.

144

Further Reading

See also novels by Virginia Driving Hawk Sneve (Sioux) and Janet Campbell Hale (Coeur d' Alene).

NORTHEAST AND SOUTHEAST

Conklin, Paul. *Choctaw Boy.* New York: Dodd, Mead, 1975. An eleven-year-old Choctaw boy living in Central Mississippi.

Henderson, Nancy and Dewey, Jane. *Circle of Life: The Miccosukee Indian Way.* New York: Messner, 1974.

Lyons, Oren. *Dog Story.* New York: Holiday House, 1973. A story about deep friendship between a boy and dog, by an Onondaga author.

Pratson, Frederick J. *Land of the Four Directions.* Old Greenwich, Ct.: Chatham Press, 1970. A photographic essay about life among Passamaquoddy, Maliseet, and Micmac Tribes of Maine and New Brunswick, Canada.

Tamarin, Alfred. *We Have Not Vanished: Eastern Indians of the United States.* Chicago: Follett, 1974. Descriptions of tribes from Maine to Florida.

PRAIRIES AND PLAINS

Ashabranner, Brent. *Morning Star, Black Sun.* New York: Dodd, Mead, 1982. Relations between the Northern Cheyenne of Montana and the U.S. government, including the tribe's recent fight to save its lands from strip-mining coal companies. Photographs by Paul Conklin.

Brill, Charles. *Indian and Free: A Contemporary Portrait of Life on a Chippewa Reservation.* Minneapolis: University of Minnesota, 1971.

Erdoes, Richard. *Native Americans: The Sioux Indians.* New York: Sterling, 1982. Contemporary Lakota life in the Dakotas.

Erdoes, Richard. *Sun Dance People: The Plains Indians, Their Past and Present.* New York: Knopf, 1972. Photographs and text.

LaPointe, Frank. *The Sioux Today.* New York: Crowell-Collier, 1972. Twenty-four stories about culture and problems of Sioux young people today, by Sioux author. Photographs by Wayne Moore.

Vizenor, Gerard. *The Everlasting Sky: New Voices from the People Named the Chippewa.* New York: Crowell-Collier, 1972. Descriptions of the Minnesota Chippewa today, by Chippewa author.

SOUTHWEST

Clark, Ann Nolan. *Circle of Seasons.* New York: Farrar, Straus, and Giroux, 1970. Ceremonies and rituals that mark and form Pueblos' year.

Elting, Mary. *The Hopi Way.* New York: Evans, 1969. Explains contemporary Hopi life, with illustrations by Hopi artist Louis Mofsie.

Erdoes, Richard. *The Native Americans: Navajos*(1978) and *Native Americans: The Pueblos* (1983). New York: Sterling.

Hirst, Stephen. *Life in a Narrow Place.* New York: McKay, 1976. The story of the Havasupai Nation who live at the bottom of the Grand Canyon.

McCarthy, T.L. *Of Mother Earth and Father Sky: A Photographic Study of Navajo Culture.* Rough Rock, Arizona: Navajo Curriculum Center, 1983.

Wood, Nancy. *Hollering Sun.* New York: Simon and Schuster, 1972. Poetry, legends, and photographs of Taos Pueblo, New Mexico.

NORTHWEST AND ALASKA

Bruemmer, Fred. *Seasons of the Eskimo.* Greenwich, Ct.: New York Graphic Society; 1971. A year in the life of an Eskimo.

Deloria, Vine, Jr. *Indians of the Pacific Northwest: From the Coming of the White Man to the Present Day.* New York: Doubleday, 1977. By a Sioux author.

Jenness, Aylette. *Dwellers of the Tundra: Life in an Alaskan Eskimo Village.* New York: Crowell-Collier, 1970. Photo essay about Makumiut, "the place of our people."

Kirk, Ruth. *David, Young Chief of the Quileutes: An American Indian Today.* New York: Harcourt, Brace and World, 1967. An eleven-year-old Quileute boy in Washington State.

Meyer, Carolyn. *Eskimos: Growing Up in a Changing Culture.* New York: Atheneum, 1977. Traditional Eskimo lifeways and the influences of dominant American culture on Eskimo people.

Senungetuk, Joseph E. *Give or Take a Century: An Eskimo Chronicle.* San Francisco: Indian Historian Press, 1971. Story of the author's family and their adjustments to non-Eskimo culture.

BIBLIOGRAPHIES

Byler, Mary Gloyne, compiler. *American Indian Authors for Young Readers: A Selected Bibliography.* New York: Association on American Indian Affairs, 1973.

Stensland, Anna Lee and Fadum, Aune F. *Literature by and about The American Indian: An Annotated Bibliography.* Urbana, Ill.: National Council of Teachers of English, 1979.

Index

148

Lumbees, 97
Lummis, 81

Maine, 106-07
Mandans, 6
Mashpee Wampanoags, 97, 107
Massachusetts, 25, 107
Maricopas, 5, 39, 64
medical doctors, 60
medicine men or women (*see* sacred healers)
Menominees, 79, 81, 109-11
Metlakatla Reservation, 11 (*see also* Tsimpshians)
Miccosukees, 7, 33, 39
Michigan, 26
Micmacs, 43
military enlistment of Indians, 3-4
Mills, William "Billy," 132
Minnesota, 25, 94, 105
Mississippi, 11, 26
Missouri, 26
Mohawks, 31, 43, 75
Momaday, N. Scott, 141
Montana, 11

Nakai, Carlos, 123
N.A.N.A. Corporation, 22
Narragansetts, 107
National Archives and Records Service, 91
National Congress of American Indians (NCAI), 136, 143
National Indian Youth Council (NIYC), 137
National Urban Indian Council, 137
Native American Public Broadcasting Corporation, 126
Native American Rights Fund (NARF), 137, 143
Native American Studies Program, 143
Navajo Code Talkers, 4
Navajo Community College, 29, 70-71
Navajos (Dinés): clothing of, 39-40; forest products of, 81; government of, 8; healers, 59; hogans of, 31, 34; jewelry of, 117-18; language of, 9, 25, 27, 70; largest tribe, 5; meaning of Diné, 2; miners, 90; newspaper of, 141; population of, 5, 73; reservation of, 11, 103; sacred site of, 45; sand paintings of, 59; schools of, 69-70; treaty with U.S. government, 92; tribal court of,

9; unemployment of, 84, weaving of, 116
Nebraska, 26, 105
New Mexico, 7, 26, 31
newspapers, 141-43
New York, 12, 105
Nez Perces, 95
Nipmucs, 7
Nisquallys, 94
Nixon, Richard, 71, 111-12, 113
North Dakota, 26, 86

Oglala Sioux, 5, 84, 87
Ohio, 26
oil, 11, 83, 90
Oklahoma, 26, 65, 105, 124
Olympic Games, 132
Oneidas, 31, 107
Onondagas, 31
oral tradition, 57, 61, 62, 66-67, 140
Oregon, 94, 95, 105, 109-10
Ortega, Paul, 123

painting, 114, 117
Paiutes, 25, 29, 45-46, 79
Papago (Tohono O'odham Nation): baskets of, 117; clothing of, 39; elder programs of, 64; irrigate crops, 79; meaning of Tohono O'odham, 2; population of, 5; reservation, size of, 11, 64; water on reservation of, 80-81
Passamaquoddies, 87, 106-07
Paugussets, 11
Pawnees, 31
Pennacooks, 97
Penobscots, 87, 106-07
performing artists, 122-27
Pimas: baskets of, 117; elder programs of, 64; irrigate crops, 79; population of, 5
Pine Ridge Sioux Reservation (*see* Oglala Sioux)
poetry, 140
Pomos, 28
population of Native Americans: in cities, 3, 5, 73; from 1890-1980, 3, 73; on reservations, 3, 5, 73; young, 3, 17, 18
Potawatomis, 91, 109
poverty, 34, 74, 84-85
powwows, 33, 37, 38, 40, 76, 133-34

150

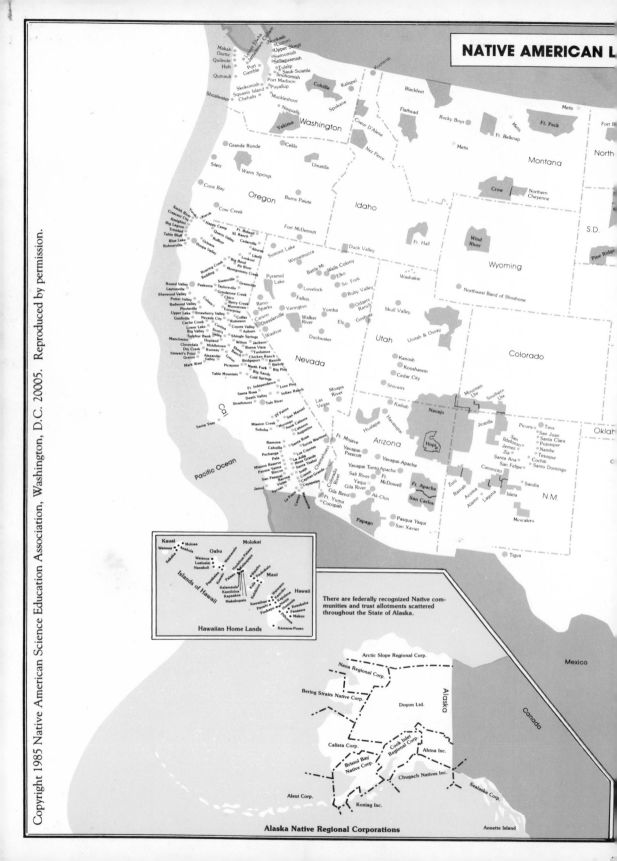

NATIVE AMERICAN L

Makah
Ozette
Quileute
Hoh
Quinault
Lower Elwha
Jamestown
S'Klallam
Nooksak
Lummi
Upper Skagit
Swinomish
Stillaguamish
Port Gamble
Tulalip
Sauk-Suiattle
Snohomish
Port Madison
Skokomish
Squaxin Island
Chehalis
Puyallup
Muckleshoot
Shoalwater
Nisqually

Colville
Kalispel
Blackfeet
Spokane
Flathead
Rocky Boys
Ft. Peck
Metis
Fort B
Coeur D'Alene
Metis
Ft. Belknap
Metis

Kootenai

Grande Ronde
Celilo
Nez Perce
Montana
North
Siletz
Umatilla
Warm Springs
Coos Bay
Burns Paiute
Idaho
Crow
Northern Cheyenne
Cow Creek
S.D.

Oregon

Smith River
Crescent City
Resighini
Big Lagoon
Trinidad
Table Bluff
Blue Lake
Rohnerville
Yurok
Karok
Happy Camp
Ft. Bidwell
XL Ranch
Cedarville
Quartz Valley
Ruffeys
Orleans
Hoopa Valley

Fort McDermitt

Ft. Hall
Wind River
Wyoming
Pine Ridge

Alturas
Likely
Lookout
Big Bend
Pit River
Montgomery Creek
Summit Lake
Winnemucca
Battle Mt
Wells Colony
Elko
So. Fork
Ruby Valley
Washakie

Roaring Creek
Redding
Greenville
Pyramid Lake
Lovelock
Northwest Band of Shoshone
Susanville
Taylorsville
Grindstone Creek
Chico
Berry Creek
Mooretown
Enterprise
Strawberry Valley
Nevada City
Colfax
Robinson
Reno-Sparks
Fallon
Yerington
Odders Ranch
Skull Valley

Paskenta

Potter Valley
Redwood Valley
Pinoleville
Upper Lake
Guidville
Cache Creek
Colusa
Carson
Washoe
Duckwater
Goshute
Unitah & Ouray

Lower Lake
Big Valley
Sulphur Bank
Manchester
Cloverdale
Dry Creek
Stewart's Point
Graton
Cortina
Scott's Valley
Auburn
Coyote Valley
Shingle Springs
Jackson
Wilton
Buena Vista
Hopland
Middletown
Sheep Ranch
Tuolumne
Rumsey
Chicken Ranch
Alexander Valley
Lytton
Bridgeport
Benton
Bishop
Big Pine
Picayune
North Fork

Colorado
Kanosh
Koosharem
Cedar City
Shivwits
Utah

Mark West
Table Mountain
Big Sandy
Cold Springs
Lone Pine
Moapa River
Kaibab
Mountain Ute
Southern Ute
Ft. Independence
Santa Rosa
Death Valley
Indian Ranch
Tule River
Las Vegas
Havasupai
Navajo
Jicarilla
Strathmore

Nevada

Santa Ynez
29 Palms
San Manuel
Hualapai
Hopi
Taos
Picuris
San Juan
San Ildefonso
Santa Clara
Pojoaque
Nambe
Tesuque
Cochiti
Santo Domingo

Mission Creek
Soboba
Morongo
Cabazon
Augustine
Ft. Mojave
Yavapai-Prescott
Arizona
Jemez
Zia
Santa Ana
San Felipe

Ramona
Cahuilla
Pechanga
Pala
Santa Rosa
Torres Martinez
Yavapai-Apache
Yavapai Tonto Apache
Canoncito
Sandia

Mission Reserve
Pauma Yaima
Rincon
La Jolla
Mesa Grande
Santa Ysabel
Salt River
Ft. McDowell
Yaqui
Ft. Apache
Zuni
Acoma
Laguna
Isleta

San Pasqual
Barona
Captain Grande
Gila River
Ramah
Alamo

Jamul
Sycuan
La Posta
Campo
Cuyapaipe
Colorado River
Ak-Chin
Ft. Apache
San Carlos
N.M.

Manzanita
Ft. Yuma
Cocopah
Gila Bend
Papago
Pasqua Yaqui
San Xavier
Mescalero

Pacific Ocean

Cal.

Tigua

Islands of Hawaii

Kauai
Waimea
Moloaa
Anahola
Molokai
Kekaha
Oahu
Waianae
Lualualei
Nanakuli
Maui
Kalamaula
Kamiloloa
Kapaakea
Makakupaia
Hawaii
Papakolea
Kewalo
Paualii
Honokaia
Keaukaha
Panaewa
Kekaha
Puukapu
Waimanu
Lalamilo
Makuu
Kamaoa-Puueo

Hawaiian Home Lands

There are federally recognized Native communities and trust allotments scattered throughout the State of Alaska.

Arctic Slope Regional Corp.
Nana Regional Corp.
Bering Straits Native Corp.
Doyon Ltd.
Alaska
Mexico
Calista Corp.
Cook Inlet Regional Corp.
Ahtna Inc.
Canada
Bristol Bay Native Corp.
Chugach Natives Inc.
Aleut Corp.
Koniag Inc.
Sealaska Corp.

Alaska Native Regional Corporations

Annette Island